THE FINAL COMMANDMENTS

LUTISHA TESAREK

TRAFFORD
PUBLISHING

This is a work of fiction. Any similarities to persons living or dead are either coincidental or fictionalized for creative purposes.

Note for Librarians: a cataloguing record for this book that includes Dewey Decimal Classification and US Library of Congress numbers is available from the Library and Archives of Canada. The complete cataloguing record can be obtained from their online database at: www.collectionscanada.ca/amicus/index-e.html
ISBN 1-4120-6736-7
Printed in Victoria, BC, Canada

Printed on paper with minimum 30% recycled fibre.
Trafford's print shop runs on "green energy" from solar, wind and other environmentally-friendly power sources.

TRAFFORD
PUBLISHING™

Offices in Canada, USA, Ireland and UK
This book was published *on-demand* in cooperation with Trafford Publishing. On-demand publishing is a unique process and service of making a book available for retail sale to the public taking advantage of on-demand manufacturing and Internet marketing. On-demand publishing includes promotions, retail sales, manufacturing, order fulfilment, accounting and collecting royalties on behalf of the author.

Book sales for North America and international:
Trafford Publishing, 6E–2333 Government St.,
Victoria, BC v8т 4р4 CANADA
phone 250 383 6864 (toll-free 1 888 232 4444)
fax 250 383 6804; email to orders@trafford.com
Book sales in Europe:
Trafford Publishing (uк) Ltd., Enterprise House, Wistaston Road Business Centre,
Wistaston Road, Crewe, Cheshire cw2 7rp UNITED KINGDOM
phone 01270 251 396 (local rate 0845 230 9601)
facsimile 01270 254 983; orders.uk@trafford.com
Order online at:
trafford.com/05-1647

10 9 8 7 6 5 4 3 2

Dedicated to

Monk Michael
St. Catherine Monastery
Sinai, Egypt

ACKNOWLEDGMENTS

This book would not be possible without the help in editing from Julie Aikins and Noreen Franklin.

Cover picture of sunrise at Mount Sinai, Egypt where Moses received the Ten Commandments

Contents

1

BACK TO THE FUTURE

"Attention, passengers on TWA flight 800 to Cairo, there has been a two-hour delay."

I smiled ruefully. What made me think this trip would be any different? A plane on time, perfect connections, someone waiting at the other end to help? Why was I allowed these extra two hours? Perhaps so I could change my mind and go back home?

I pulled out the envelope and examined it again. There was no return address, just the Par Avion print at the top left corner. On the right, two thirty-five piaster stamps from Egypt with a picture of a famous mosque. Inside, the same piece of paper that I had looked at five days ago, fourteen simple words. "It is time. Come to the Monastery and Suliman will bring you to me." At the bottom was no "St. Catherine Monastery Sinai" official seal, no title " The Secretary of the Monastery," just a simple signature, Monk Arsenios.

I still had almost two hours to go, enough time to get my bags off the plane. It wouldn't be the first time I've changed my mind. Once, while visiting my sister in Kansas, I decided to move back from Hawaii. I left my two children with her and took the train to California to catch a plane to go back to pack our belongings. At the second stop, I got off the train and called a friend to come pick me up. Something told me it wasn't the right time to leave Hawaii. Needless to say, my sister was surprised to see me on her doorstep the next morning. I haven't surprised her since, because she just assumes I have no common sense.

No one could blame me now if I didn't go to Egypt. After all, it was a commitment I made over ten years ago, even if it was to a priest. People make these commitments without considering the future, like at the YWCA camp when we were kids. We pricked our fingers and became blood sisters, promising to meet in twenty years and compare our lives. No one ever showed up. Besides, who in their right mind would fly seventeen thousand miles, halfway around the world, with no phone number or location, to meet someone who hadn't communicated or been seen for over ten years?

As my sister might comment, "Someone without common sense."

So, here I was, headed for my fourth trip to one of the holiest places on earth. The place where Moses received the Ten Commandments. At the foot of Mount Moussa sets St. Catherine Monastery, which was built around the Burning Bush. A Greek Orthodox Monastery, in an Arab speaking land, on a Jewish site, in the country of Egypt. It is probably the most isolated place for religious pilgrimages because of its location. A journey from Cairo took eight days by foot and camel in the fourteenth century. Its isolation is also one of the reasons it holds the second largest collection of religious and historical documents, next to the Vatican's. The monastery was spared during the inquisitions.

I reminisced about my longstanding connection to the Monastery. The first time, we arrived late at night, so I did not see the beauty of the Monastery. We were going to Petra by ferry over the Sea of Aqaba to Jordan. My first meeting with Monk Arsenios was at breakfast. His hearty laugh and sparkling eyes were magnetic. As we left, he told me I would be returning, but at that point in my life, I couldn't imagine making that dreadful drive through the desert again.

The second visit was a year later when my former roommate from the University of Hawaii came to spend a month with me. We were going for the weekend to climb to the top of Mount Moussa where Moses had received the Ten Commandants.

We arrived at dusk, and the sunset was breathtaking. The air was so clear and fresh. Just imagine stepping out of a smoke-filled, noisy, crowded, smelly bus onto the sand where Moses walked, where there was no pollution or noise, just the whisper of the wind.

During the weekend, I was invited to stay as their guest to set up their computer system. I had been working for the Library of Congress at the American Embassy in Cairo. The Library of Congress had microfilmed much of the Monastery's collection back in 1956.

What began as a business project lasting only a few days turned out to be a months-long spiritual journey for which I wasn't prepared. I was supposed to be Monk Arsenios' computer teacher, and instead, he ended up being my spiritual guide.

He gave me a rare glimpse into their most precious collections. The Monastery is actually the legal owner of the oldest bible in the world, the Codex Syriacus from the fifth Century. It was borrowed in 1865 by a German scholar on behalf of the Russian Czar for research and never returned. Disappearing during the Russian revolution, it showed up again in 1933. The British Museum purchased it from the Soviets. The Museum refused to return it, even after the Monastery offered to reimburse them for the bible. Their icon collection consists of over two thousand, twelve of which are the rarest and oldest icons of the sixth century.

During Israel's occupation of the Sinai, two huge generators were installed for the Monastery. We could only use electricity for two hours a night, which was when I was able to work. During the time the electricity was off, Monk Arsenios discussed the state of my soul and ended every conversation by saying, " Natasha, how is your material life working out for you?" I don't think he realized I didn't have a material life. I had a couple of boxes stored in the States and that was it. He kept asking when I was going to be ready to fulfill my obligation on earth. I couldn't comprehend what he was saying.

"Each person has a duty in his lifetime to use his talents to better the planet." I laughed and said, "That's not me! I have no talent." "Yes you have, Natasha! Don't ever belittle yourself again," he said, in a very stern voice, as if he was mad at me.

THE FINAL COMMANDMENTS

I wanted to apologize, but I didn't know what for. I couldn't stand the thought of him being cross with me.

"Are you not aware of the power of your words? You create tomorrow with your words and thoughts today. Do you know the two most powerful words in the world?" He was very serious, I could see that. I just shook my head no. He quoted the bible verse when Moses was at the Burning Bush and asked God who he was. God responded, "I AM that I AM." God's name is I AM, and any time you invoke these words, you are asking God for something. You will see his name I AM in hieroglyphs on all the tombs."

He continued, "Religions have become like governments; they don't want the common person to realize this power, and they want to make people believe they have to come to church for God. God is right there inside you, waiting for you to just ask, and he will deliver. This is why it upsets me so when I hear the tourist walking around saying, 'I'm so tired.' They are bringing on the state of being tired by asking the universe for it. "Are you familiar with manifesting?"

I shook my head. He laughed and said we really had many lessons ahead of us. "You give me homework, and I give you homework." He smiled and started writing. "I want you to write down all your talents, and what you wish to contribute to this world in your lifetime." He handed me my homework, and I just stared at it.

At our next meeting, I explained to Monk Arsenios I hadn't really studied the bible on a scholarly basis. He laughed and said, "If you had, it would have been a waste of time. Many people believe all statements in the bible are literally true. Religion has been used all through the centuries, just as governments are using it to their benefit. Consider this. It consists of sixty-six different books, composed by many different writers, in three different languages. Writers of almost every social rank, statesmen and peasants, kings, herdsmen, fishermen, priests, taxgatherers, educated and uneducated, Jews and Gentiles. Most were unknown to each other in a period of sixteen hundred years, centering on the subject of man's redemption. There was a break of four hundred years between the Old Testament and the New."

He went on to explain the Nicaea Council of 325 AD convened mortal men to decide which writings would be accepted into the bible, changing the day of worship from Saturday to Sunday, changing Jesus' birthday to December 25th, and introducing Easter, which used to be a pagan worship called "Feast of Ishtar." This is why Egypt has three different dates for Christmas; Coptic, Greek and Christian. Many books were left out. If it hadn't been for the discovery of the Dead Sea Scrolls and the papyrus scrolls from the Nag Hammadi Library, we might have never realized how much was missing." Our next meetings covered things I'd never heard of before. He spoke of the Akashic Records, which is a universal record of every thought, action and word spoken.

My mind staggered at all of this new information. I began to think I was intentionally brought into this fold of selected people for this project because of my background with libraries. The old saying, "in the right place at the right time" began to take on new meaning.

Although most people have heard of Atlantis, I had always thought of it as a myth. Monk Arsenios explained there was a prehistoric existence of the lost civilization of Atlantis, which paralleled Plato's account in many respects, such as the achievement of a higher civilization, followed by cataclysm and destruction. The reason for the destruction of Atlantis was the misapplication of power. Before the destruction of Atlantis around 10,500 BCE, the Atlanteans created three repositories for the records of their culture and the history of humanity.

These records were deposited in a "hall of records" in Egypt, in Tibet, and in Central America. The first storage place in Egypt was the Pyramids. Due to diggings and research round the Pyramids, they were then moved to the Alexandria Library, which, at that time, was the depository of all knowledge. Even Jesus studied there nearly million manuscripts from the entire civilized world. It even had Aristotle's own private collection. All visitors were required to surrender all books and scrolls, which was swiftly copied by official scribes. The library kept the originals and send the copies to the owners. Even Jesus DNA was stored and saved for questions, which would be bought up centuries later. When the fire occurred at the library, these records were moved to the desert for safekeeping. The records included what Monk Arsenios called the final commandments, universal laws based on energy. They dealt with the soul of each person in connection with the universal power, and had nothing to do with religion.

My time at St. Catherine's was the most peaceful time I had ever known. Every time I went for a walk, I thought, "These could be the exact steps that Moses took." In this location and atmosphere, one couldn't help but start thinking on a spiritual level.

2

PERSONAL STORY

The two-hour delay gave me time to reflect, once again, in how different I was from the girl who had visited that first time. So often, I thought, "Oh, if only I knew then what I know now."

Then I would smile and remind myself what Monk Arsenios told me, "Natasha, you had to live what you lived then to become what you are now."

Now that I was aware of the ancient laws based on universal energy, I could clearly see how they had impacted my life.

Looking back, I realized my life didn't really start until I was eighteen. Growing up was always a struggle and nothing I wanted to remember. We traveled around until my family split up. My brother went to work with my father at a very early

THE FINAL COMMANDMENTS

age, my sister went out to live with an aunt in California, and I stayed with mother and frequently changing stepfathers.

Now, I realized, these were the building blocks for my life, no matter how painful they were. One of the Universal Laws definitely applied to those years: Law of wisdom – you seem to learn fastest through pain.

Sometimes I wonder what my life would have been if I'd been born two generations earlier. Another law; Law of Magnetic Affinity, you choose astrological time and date of birth, choose lessons to be learned, choose parents, strengths, and weakness. My father's side was Attorneys and Judges. It seems to go down hill after that. Just spoiled adults with a good name, but not the backbone to carry on the family tradition. The Law of Denial; refuse to take responsibility, do not live up to your potential would seem to fit here.

For people who might be complaining about not having material goods, or support from their family, I say look on it as a blessing. For this will be the time to build character. Plus the best part is, you know it only last for a certain amount of years, after that, you make your own rules. A hard lesson I learned is my parents couldn't teach me something they don't know or understand. This is why knowledge is so important.

My mother had to leave school at an early age as her parents died and she was left to live with and older married sister. From her I learned honesty and the principle of hard work. Her dream was always a man to take care of her, but of course it always worked out just the opposite. She's what's referred to in social terms as the "rescuer." She couldn't instill in me dreams and setting goals, as she was always in survival mode. This could be referred to as the Law of Restriction; you cannot create anything higher than your level of understanding.

From my Father I learned the carefree, ego aspects of life. He would come through every few years with a new flashy car, which I was allowed to drive, and we'd catch a plan and fly someplace.

Now I realize how fortunate I was, being born with the wrong spoon in my mouth. To struggle for everything you get builds the character, and makes you appreciate everything when you do receive it.

I always dreamed of being Scarlet, coming down the spiral staircase for my coming out party. In reality, the coming out party, graduation from high school, was one of my saddest days. It started with our last pep rally assembly, where all our classmates gathered for the last time. I cried from the depths of my heart with pain. I knew this was going to be the last day of fun in my life! My life was over! I couldn't afford college and probably didn't have the grades. For me, school was a social event, full of games and parties, the learning part of it was only irritating tests and books to carry.

Even my graduation night told me I was doomed. A tornado wiped out a town just twenty miles away. My sister had brought her baby, who wasn't feeling well, and he screamed throughout the ceremony. My mother had on a new crepe dress, which had shrunk up above her knees and was ruined. To top the evening off, when we got home, a tree fell on Mom's car. In spite of all that, it meant so much for my family to be there, because I was the first one in our family to graduate from high school.

At the age of sixteen I fell in love for the first time. Your first love is the biggest lesson you'll ever have, and the most painful. This would be the Law of Attraction; where your attention goes, energy flows. This is so true, my whole life was about him. He went in the service, so the relationship was through correspondence and his leaves. It was not a peaceful, calm relationship, but an emotional roller coaster. Hopefully a person matures and doesn't have to go through that again, although there are some people that picks the same type of person, with the same lesson each time. The law of Self worth; you only attract to you that which you feel worthy of would fit here. Thankfully I've learned my lessons well, and each relationship is a new learning experience. He joined the marines, and we had been corresponding for two years. He would be back from Japan soon and we would reunite in California.

After graduation, one of my family friends who had moved to California invited me to come and live with them. Since I had only traveled to four of the Midwest states, this sounded like a great adventure. I traveled on the Super Chief train to Los Angeles Union Station. It was the first time another Universal Law applied to me: the law of New Beginnings: a major life changing time comes with a break in brain patterns. It was first experience of new beginnings, the first of what would become several pivotal points in my life. My adventures were about to begin!

At Long Beach, I saw a big gray battleship in the ocean and immediately realized I wanted to travel and see the entire world. One that has always lived by the ocean cannot imagine the impact of seeing an ocean for the first time. Ah! Another Universal Law: the law of Manifestation: what begins as a thought, an idea, creates your reality.

Eventually, I moved to an all girls' residence close to a hospital, where many of the occupants were nurses and professional people. It was a safe haven for women back in the fifties who had come to the big city. I landed a job. When I mentioned to some of the girls at work that I was looking for a place closer to my job, one of the girls, Joan, suggested Ivy Terrace.

When I saw the place I was in awe! It had a pool, a common area downstairs where suitors could call, a kitchen on each floor, and a bedroom which was shared with a roommate.

How well I remember Ms. Machete interviewing me! She was a large matronly looking woman whose hair was pulled back in a bun and whose huge bossism hung down to her belt. She seemed impressed that I was from the Midwest, had a job, and didn't drink or smoke.

"Great" she said, "I have a lovely Mormon girl who wants a roommate who doesn't smoke." My heart sank! At that time I was thinking Moslem, with the headscarf. The following day, I told Joan I had been accepted at Ivy Terrace.

"Where will you be staying?" she asked.

"I'll be in 208."

Then she answered quietly "That's my room."

I blurted out, "That can't be! She says there's a nice Mormon girl staying there."

She looked me straight in the eyes and said, "I'm Mormon."

My mouth dropped. I couldn't figure out which would be worse, living with a foreigner wearing a scarf or someone who would be reporting at work what time I got in at night!

Joan and I became the best of friends; I even introduced her to her husband. At Ivy Terrace was the first time I learned about religions. One of the girls was Jewish, three were Catholic. Growing up as a hard shell Baptist, I had been taught other religions were not based on truth. I couldn't believe that my new diverse friends wouldn't be saved because they had different beliefs than I did. That early ability to question previously taught doctrine led me to understand another Universal Law, the law of Soul evolution: everyone on earth shares the goal of soul evolution, we learn from our disharmony and failure.

That Universal Law also applied to my personal life, although I wouldn't realize it until years later, until my stay at St. Catherine's.

In Los Angeles, I worked two jobs and went to Night College. My boyfriend, Paul, returned from the service. I lost my virginity, we fought, made up, fought, and finally broke up. I was nineteen years old and again was certain that my life was over, there was nothing left for me.

The one good thing that did come out of this was I met and married the best human being I have yet to meet. When Paul and I fought by letter, one of his Marine friends would write to me to help us to make up. After Paul and I broke up, William and I kept writing as friends, and when he came back from Hawaii to San Diego, we finally met in person and began dating. William was Paul's complete opposite. He had no ego to deal with, was truthful and didn't drink or smoke. He was just a wonderful human being, and even now, the best human being I know. Not drinking was important to me, as my mother always married alcoholics and I swore I wouldn't include an alcoholic in my life. In my mind, the alcohol led to divorce; therefore, I reasoned, no alcohol, no divorce. I did not want to divorce and remarry in the same pattern as my mother.

William and I married, had two children, ready to live happily every after with the white picket fence. Then my mother died.

Once, my mother visited us in California and said to me, "You are so lucky, you have the perfect man. Why couldn't I have met someone like that?"

When I recalled that conversation now, I saw that I had applied the law of Manifestation: what begins as a thought creates your reality. These laws work for your good or bad with free will. When my mother uttered that statement, I turned it into a reality, although at the time I didn't realize I was applying a Universal Law to my life. My mother didn't have a good husband, so I didn't deserve one either.

William and I eventually got a divorce for no good reason, I realize, with regret, now. William ended up marring a wonderful woman, and has the perfect life with the picket fence. His wife is a loving and caring person, whose gentle, loving spirit has helped me forgive myself for our marital breakup.

I moved with the two children to Honolulu, and began another phase of my life. It was a wonderful place to raise children, I thought. I was giving the children travel and adventure, something I never had. I did not realize then that they really wanted a secure environment and normal home.

My growth at this time certainly wasn't spiritual, or even academic. I would have to classify it as a cultural life experience. I'd never been in contact with Asians or Polynesians. This was a totally new discovery for me. I admired the way everyone got along, even with there diverse religions and cultures. People respected each other's thoughts and beliefs, which reminded me of a joke someone once told me about a Chinese man at the cemetery placing rice cakes and other food on his loved one's grave, which is their tradition. A person from the mainland was placing flowers one his loved one's grave. The mainlander looked over and amusingly asked the Chinese man when his friend was coming up to eat the food. Very politely he answered, "The same time your friend comes up to smell your flowers."

I began incorporating traits from each of the cultures. The Japanese were the largest population, and held most of the government positions. The Chinese were the bankers, and the Hawaiians were the heart of the islands.

I worked for one of the largest landowners in the island, a young Chinese man with a very mild manner. Most evenings after work we went for pupu's, local food treats, in the local places with the group from work. I was accepted in this social circle because of whom I worked for. Mr. Fong was married to a beautiful Chinese wife from a well-to-do family. Like most of the wealthy men, he had a girlfriend also. She was a beautiful Japanese woman named Akiko and worked for one of his best friends at a bank he owned.

One night I ended up on the stage with Don Ho dancing the hula. I was accepted by the entertainers and became part of the Hawaiian Mongoose Pack! The Mongoose Pack consisted of the top entertainers in the island, plus a couple of hotel owners. Here was another stage of my life where a Universal Law applied, the law of Reflection: traits you respond to in others, you recognize in yourself. This law could be the same as 'birds of a feather flock together." At this stage in my life my interest was in having fun and socializing.

Partying was the accepted social practice. The bankers and the businessmen cut out about midnight, leaving the rest of use to pub-crawl until all the clubs closed at 4 A.M.

One evening a drink was sent to my table commenting on how much he enjoyed my dance. Although I was accepted in the circle, you do not invite a stranger to the table. When I went over to thank him, I noticed sadness in his eyes. It was like he was a lost puppy setting in the middle of the road. When I turned to leave, he took my hand gently and asked if I cared to have a bowl of saimin with him when the show closed. At that time Waikiki was like a community, you were safe no matter where you went. I knew I couldn't invite him to the table, so I told him about a saimin stand two blocks away and I'd meet him there at 2 A.M.

When I saw him waiting at the table, I was struck by the realization that I felt like I had known him forever. Once again, looking back, I can see the Universal Laws at work. The law of Psychometric Influences says when two people come in contact, mental connection contact and influence. We started talking as if we had known each other all our life. Words just flowed off my tongue. He was a very tall, handsome, educated foreigner who seemed to know everything about the world. I was in awe of him. He mentioned he was raised in the Cameroon's, and I mentioned something about Asia.

He politely stated, "You're thinking of Cambodia. The Cameroon's is in West Africa."

I thought of all the history classes I had sat through and paid no attention. As he talked, I became aware of the real lack of my education. Hawaii now seemed like a very small place. Our cultural, economic, and religious backgrounds were complete opposites. He was on a ship doing scientific research which he couldn't talk about. We walked on the beach, sat in the sand and talked until sunrise. We agreed to dinner and a movie the next night.

THE FINAL COMMANDMENTS

Tomaso seemed so sad. When we went to see "The Sound of Music," his only comment was, "What is good about a family who has to leave their country because a hostile government takes it over?"

Tomaso's father was actually a wealthy industrialist in Russia when the revolution began. He could stay and be killed or leave. His father left and went to Prague, Czechoslovakia, where he met his mother Maika, of the same social standing he was. They were married and had two sons. When they returned from a cruise the Germans took their original passports and gave them German ones. Feeling threatened, they melted down their gold, and transferred out what money they could, and moved to the French Cameroon's in West Africa.

They settled on a tong oil and coffee plantation miles from civilization. Their nearest neighbors, a man named Pip from Hawaii and a lady from England, lived fifty miles away. Tomaso's father and Pip's wife ran off together to South Africa, and Tomaso's mother and Pip eventually got married.

After World War II the French Cameroon's gained their independence, and the natives retaliated against the white plantation owners by hacking them to pieces with machetes. When Tomaso was sixteen, his family moved to Florida to start an orchard grove there. His life of privilege just kept deteriorating; from wealthy industrialist in Europe, to plantation owners in Africa, to orchard growers in America, then to an ordinary citizen in a foreign land. Tomaso longed for those times on the plantation, where they were the rulers of their entire domain. The law of Karma basically says what goes around comes around. When I met him, Tomaso was at the complete other end of the spectrum, being told what to do by others.

Tomaso and I enjoyed doing things as a family. He taught the children and me to play chess. He was always telling the children stories of Africa and his travels. While he was away at sea, I started reading to become more aware of the world. I knew I wanted to spend my life with him and give the children the advantage to travel the world. One of the books I read stated that one's thoughts could influence actions, so I wrote my name as his wife, "Mrs. Natasha Niska," one hundred times as the book had instructed.

Once, Tomaso's ship was over a week late. I knew only a rough estimate each time of about how long his ship would be out, but usually I could guess within a week of when it was due in port. One of the wives called and asked if I had news from Tomaso. It was already a week late. She was very concerned. In my first days at work for Mr. Fong, I had gone to lunch a couple of times with a Federal Judge. I called him and invited him to lunch again. After the niceties, he laughed and said, "I hear you've left The Mongoose Pack and are now with the scientists." I was surprised he had kept up with my social life. He laughed and commented that everyone knew everyone else's business on a small island.

I mentioned that Tomaso's ship was late and said to him, "All I know is what they're doing is classified, and they're under the direct orders of Secretary of Defense Robert McNamara."

The color drained from his face. He didn't blink an eye, and just kept eating. "I'll check into it for you and see what I can find out," he said.

About nine, I heard a knock at the door. The second knock let me know it was to be answered. I opened it a crack, and found a sober looking man, in an exceptional expensive suit, flashing a badge at me. He asked me who else knew about my lunch with Judge T. S. Goo. I told him I hadn't mentioned it to anyone. He gave me a piece of paper with a name and phone number on it and instructed me to give it to the wife of the other man on Tomaso's ship, then warned me not to mention this conversation with anyone. When I looked up from the piece of paper, he had disappeared down the driveway.

Almost two weeks before the ship showed up, and Tomaso was in an unusually bitter mood about the government and the power they had over people. He said he was ready to get off the ship and didn't know where he would go next. I just kept writing Mrs. Natasha Niska 100 hundred times.

Tomaso said this would be his last trip, he had a contract with them, but didn't like Hawaii. "There's a big world out there to be seen. Are you brave enough to explore it? Think about it while I'm gone." My heart skipped a beat at the thought of being with him, and having the children experience new places instead of just read about it.

The ship went out again while I waited.

About three in the morning one morning, the phone rang. My heart sank, expecting bad news. I picked up the phone shaking. "Hello," I said in a weak voice.

"Hello, dear heart, can you come and pick me up at Hickman Air Force Base?" It was Tomaso! He was back and in one piece. I had a live in sitter, so I woke her and told her where I was going.

I hardly recognized Tomaso. He had let his hair grow and had a beard; he looked like a hermit! When he took me in his arms every care in the world melted away. It didn't matter where we lived, as long as we were together. We went to breakfast, but discussed nothing about why he was here and the ship was still out. He went to bed and fell right to sleep. I went on to work, wondering what story I would hear that evening.

After dinner we sat on the lanai, and the story came out. They had been tracking a Russian Trawler they figured was a spy ship. The United States government wouldn't let them come in as they might lose it. They had run out of food and ships diverted to give them supplies. They were close enough to one of the islands to stop for refueling without losing sight of the trawler. The employees were allowed to get off and buy a few staples. When it was time to get board, Tomaso refused. His supervisor ordered him back on the ship. He told the supervisor, "I'm not in the military, but with a private contractor. You cannot make me get back on that ship."

The ship had to leave. There was no authority on the atoll. The supervisor threatened him with prison. Tomaso just smiled at him and said, "You know, if you take me to any sort of court, you'll have to tell them what we were doing, and I don't think our government would be too pleased about that." The gangplank was going up. The supervisor jumped on at the last minute shouting threats and obscenities at Tomaso. Tomaso just stood there smiling, waving goodbye to the ship.

Just as we were finishing dessert there was a loud knock at the door. The man in the expensive suit asked, "May I speak with Mr. Tomaso Niska in private please?" I let them speak on the lanai as I went to the kitchen to wash the dishes. It seemed like an eternity had passed when Tomaso came in and offered to help with the dishes.

That night right before we went to sleep he said in a somber voice, "I was serious about leaving Hawaii. How attached are you to the islands? After the ship docks and I get my things off, I'll be moving on. Do you want to go with me?" I didn't have to think very long to answer. I just couldn't imagine being without Tomaso.

In a few weeks the ship was due in port. We were there to greet it. We stood with all the wives waiting for the gangplank to come down, and the men to clear customs. They all greeted Tomaso as a hero, and said they wished they had the courage to walk off with him. Apparently there was a shift in management's thinking, and they believed that brought the ship back earlier than planned. In fact, the supervisor was instructed to ask Tomaso to come back on the ship and go to dry dock with them in Washington. Apparently they were scared of what he'd say and had no idea what he would do after he left the ship.

We went night clubbing for the last time to say goodbye to my friends. Don Ho's record had just come out and made the Top Ten. He autographed a copy for me, and said, "So the scientist is stealing you away from us? You'll be back, I know that for a fact!"

The ship had left, and the children and I were headed for the airport. Islanders make sure "Aloha!" comes with tears! Leis were stacked up to my eyeballs, and I sat on the plane sobbing like someone who had just lost their most precious possessions. A very important part of my life was ending, and I knew I would never have those carefree days again. It took me almost ten minutes to stop crying, and then when we flew over Diamond Head, the sobbing started all over again.

We stayed with my old roommate from Ivy Terrace until time for the ship to come in. Tomaso's supervisor still had not forgiven him for getting off the ship without punishment. The ship was going to Florida after dry-dock, so I would drive out there with the kids and meet the ship. The ship was based out of Patrick Air Force Base. He figured he might get a job with the space program out there. We had taken a week's vacation and gone to the mountains. We saw some of the crew Saturday when we returned, and they had told us the ship had to move up its departure to Sunday in order to get through the Panama Canal on time. Since Tomaso wasn't supposed to report back till Monday, he asked the crew not to mention they had seen him. When he reported on Monday, the ship had left. The same Supervisor was furious, but couldn't do a thing. Tomaso took more vacation time, and we drove together to Florida.

When we arrived in Florida the ship wouldn't be in for a few weeks. Tomaso's parents lived in Tallahassee. We were married at their lovely orchard in a quiet ceremony.

Patrick Air Force Base sent him downrange to a missile tracking station to wait for the ship to come into port. The children and I were left in Coco Beach to wait for Tomaso to return. He came back one day before the ship arrived. He had told me how pleasant Turks and Caicos Island was. He wanted us to go down there. Hadn't I just told myself it didn't matter where we were, as long as we were together? But I had just come from Hawaii, the most beautiful place on earth. This island was six miles long, and one mile wide. Nothing grew there. Most of the people didn't have electricity. There was no shopping, and a food supply boat came in every six weeks. I encountered firsthand the Law of Fearful confrontation: if you fear doing something, do it anyway, you'll do a mental flip. We would move.

THE FINAL COMMANDMENTS

When the ship pulled in, Tomaso was standing on the dock, waving. The supervisor was so angry he couldn't speak. He yelled at Tomaso, "You're not coming back on this ship!"

"I know, I'm going down range to Grand Turk," he replied.

3

TURKS AND CAICOS ISLANDS,
BRITISH WEST INDIES

We were scheduled to arrive in Grand Turk around 2:30 P.M. It was the first chain of islands past the Bahamas, about 650 miles south of the Bahamas. The water was so clear, it was a greenish color instead of the blue of Hawaii. Finally I saw a small atoll in the water. Surely this was too small to be lived on! It was all sand, with what looked like weeds at one end. They turned out to be mangroves. In the middle was what looked like a little bump in the sand. That was the highest point on the island, the T-Building as we later learned the locals referred to it, top secret. The plane was small, with two propellers humming all the way. When we got closer, I could see what looked like hundreds of people lining both

THE FINAL COMMANDMENTS

sides of the narrow runway. Later on I realized this was the big event of the week. People would be bringing back treats for their friends and news from America.

I had worn a navy blue two piece outfit with white gloves and a hat. I can just imagine what they thought of me! But to my surprise, the sixty by eighty-foot immigration shed was quite formal also. The Chief of Police had on white gloves also.

"Passports please" he very curtly demanded. "Return ticket?"

"I don't have one, I'm going to live here." The shed became absolutely quiet.

"Step to the side please." I moved to the side with the children on either side of me and stood, for what seemed like hours. People pressed past me, arguing about the cost of goods they brought through customs.

Finally an Air Force gentleman in a blue uniform pressed through and shouted, "Andy, sorry I'm late. Here is the paperwork for the lady and her two children."

"Fine, give it to me so they can clear their belongings and make more room." I thought he was rude. He would end up being Tomaso's best friend while we were on the island.

"Good afternoon, Natasha, I'm Captain Bill Davler, sorry I'm late. Please, come with me."

I followed him outside, hoping for some relief from the heat. The breeze was marvelous. It reminded me of Hawaii for a moment.

"Where is Tomaso?" I asked, thinking he should already have been here.

"We have a launch today, so he probably won't be off the hill for another twenty-four hours, depending on how long a hold they have." I didn't understand a word he said.

A high pitched woman started yelling at Capt. Davler, waving him over to her. To me, she said, "Hello, how are you? I left some sheets and schedule of events in your apartment, and if you need anything else just give me a ring. I have a telephone, and since my husband is the supervisor, we also have a base phone. Oh, I forgot, you won't have a phone, but you can walk one block to the Cable and Wireless and they will know how to contact me." In just a couple of sentences, she had let me know how important she was, and probably all requests would have to go through her. I knew already with a wife like that, Tomaso would not like the supervisor.

We were driven to a two story concrete structure known as the Grey Apartments, and helped with our belongings to the second floor. So there we sat, boxes surrounding us, hungry, with no food, or pots and pans. Our boxes mailed to the base through MATS hadn't arrived yet. The kids insisted we go out for a swim. I found their suits and we went for a walk.

I found the Cable and Wireless and asked about a grocery store. The man there laughed out loud, then realized I was serious. "Sorry, Timco closes about 3:30 P.M., and the fresh things come with frozen meat every six weeks. You just missed that. Every once in a while we'll have a Haitian boat come with mangos and bananas. You just come off the plane?" The children were whispering to me to find out were the restaurant was. "I see the children are hungry? There are no restaurants on Grand Turk Island. Just wait a minute, and let me make a phone call."

THE FINAL COMMANDMENTS

I heard him whispering into the phone. He turned to me and said, "We have a Turks Head Inn with two rooms in it for dignitaries visiting the island. The innkeeper is a jolly English lady and has some things in the refrigerator she will share with you. It's only a block farther down, and her name is Julie. She's expecting you." I thanked him for his kindness, and we took off for the most pleasant evening.

Julie was waiting for us at the gate, with a martini in hand. I had to look up at her, as she was over six feet tall, with a very deep voice. "Welcome, welcome, to our island. We had a pleasant meal in a beautiful courtyard. While we ate, she drank. By her fourth martini, she was giving me all the gossip. The big excitement was the Queen was coming on the Britannia, so all the Brits were planning a big gala for here entertainment. This was her fourth martini, so we got down to who was sleeping with whom. Then on to the gay Administrator, who wore a tiny, tiny bikini and was surrounded by young black local boys on the beach. The resident celebrity use to play with the musical group from England called the Animals. His family sent him down here hoping he'd forget the rock and roll scene. He worked for Barclays' Bank. It appears when someone in the diplomat core misbehaves they are shipped off to an island where they can't embarrass the family. Apparently she had to be invited to the British parties, since Her Majesty's Government hired her. But she hadn't made it to the American list. I knew we were going to be good friends. Now I know someone who has a phone, putting me on the A list.

Next day I went to Timco, bought cans of food and a can opener, and we survived for two days till Tomaso showed up. He was glad I hadn't taken any handouts from Angie, the supervisor's wife. He had already had a run-in with her. I was to stay out of that loop. He didn't mind the supervisor, seemed like a decent fellow. He just couldn't stand him being henpecked. Tomaso got along better with the Navy men than his coworkers.

Turks & Caicos Islands was an unusual situation. The island was actually owned by the British, but the pounds were Jamaican. The islands only source of income was selling stamps, and making salt. They leased out each end of the Grand Turk to the American government. One end was the base where our men worked. It had to be an official military base under the contract, so they had an American Air Force Captain for show. The contracts were from companies like RCA and PanAm. The wives could come at their own expense, and we had mail privileges. The Navy base was top secret, no family members. About 100 Navy personnel were stationed there. They had a PX that they let us use. I always wondered what the people filling there orders thought when they received the order for Kotex from an all-male base. The bases were a contract to pay back money from England to the United States for World War II debts. America seems to always make money on wars.

I didn't realize until we lived on Grand Turk Island how much Tomaso drank. We would go to the movie, and he would set with the guys and drink. When the movie was over, he'd stay and drink, but I had to take the kid's home for school the next day.

When Tomaso found out the Chief of Police had served for His Majesty Service in Africa, the bond became so strong that every non-working moment was spent together. They both had the same drinking habits and the need for adventure. This and

THE FINAL COMMANDMENTS

the bond with Julie from the Turks Head Inn put us in the British social circle, which was a complete irritant to Angie, the supervisor's social climber wife.

We spent five years on this small island with only a few people having electricity. There was no TV, no shopping, and no running water. A catch basin was used for water, and pump boys would come to pump water each morning. We'd get potable water from the base in a five-gallon jug. We used a kerosene stove and refrigerator. Mail came once a week; the food supply came every six weeks.

Perhaps because we were missing the usual entertainment, we created our own. There was the usual exchange of dinner parties, eight to twelve people, with strict British social protocol, and occasionally one of the visiting celebrities, like Jacque Costeau on the Calypso. Even John Glenn was brought to Grand Turk for a medical checkup and post flight de-briefing after his historic three-orbit space flight in 1962. Many years later it would become the playground for the rich and famous; like Jerry Seinfield for his honeymoon, and Ben Affleck's marriage. We could have bought a piece of beach property for $500, as long as we built a home on it in five years. Now a Club Med is on the property! The table would be set with the best linen, china, crystal, and dinner meant good food and excellent conversation. The women would excuse themselves after dinner and go into the parlor for more conversation, while the men stayed and had their smoke. I discovered that true conversation is not about illness, the most recent clothing purchase, or any number of other mundane things. In this circle of international people, conversation meant voicing an opinion on a matter of local, national, or world importance that had required personal study. Simply repeating another's point of view to maintain interest was not good enough. Once again, I became painfully aware that my education was greatly lacking.

Once a month was the extravaganza party, based on a theme, with entertainment, and of course a great meal centered around the theme. For one party we painted the house. The Navy men had found some paint and were painting the house when a surprise inspection of the Navy base was announced. Some high-ranking Navy official came driving down Front Street while two Navy men painted our civilian house with Navy paint! The vehicle drivers pointed out how beautiful the view of the water was and kept the inspector's attention away from the house!

Once we held a Playboy party, and once we set the ocean on fire. The grand finale for that party was to light two barrels of oil that had been dumped into the ocean in front of the beach. The Administrator was very unhappy when he saw the beach all lit up from the ocean side.

A big change came when I became pregnant. Americans went to the United States to have their children, and many of the Brits went back to England. I was the only American to give birth on the island.

It was quite an experience. The Doctor didn't even do the delivery, the Matron did. There was no medicine for pain, it was all natural. The children came by horse and bicycle. Tomaso was there through the delivery, and back then men didn't go into the delivery room. I managed it without missing one party! I knew Tomaso would not permit me to get out the same day I had the baby, so I had the children bring me some clothes, and the Navy picked me up and dropped me at the Matron's party. Then I was driven back to the hospital after the party.

Andy and Tomaso's drinking spiraled out of hand. They burned each other's arms with cigarettes, yelling, "Put it there mate!"

They planned a fake break-in of the security system in a drunken stupor and got fired on by the night guards. The Captain found them at the edge of the water covered with blood from coral cuts as they dodged the bullets.

"Constable Anderson, what the hell are you doing here? That was live ammunition!"

Tomaso and Andy's behavior was borderline acceptable. Andy's wife, the British Government, and the Captain at our base put a damper on their relationship. Tomaso was lost without his mischief-making sidekick. Life was no fun if you had to obey the rules. He didn't like the idea of the Captain being able to tell him how to behave.

He wanted to leave, get his pilot's license, purchase a plane, and then return to give flying lessons. There was plenty of money on the island and no place for the men to spend it. He would have a good clientele base. Also there would always be freight to fly from one island to another.

The islanders were wondering what all the noise was about. Some had even wondered if it was voodoo punishment for the island for letting foreigners have bases. The real religion on the islands is Voodoo, although everyone professed to be Christian. After this the Voodoo Priest Maurice DeBay had much prestige, as he had said for many years evil spirits were at both ends of the island. This was his proof. Later on when I started studying different religions I understood how the priest had so much control over the people. The Law of Self-Truth; truth is what works for you. Be careful what you accept.

I had an occasion to meet the Voodoo Priest because of a problem concerning my maid. Each culture is so different. She had two children, wasn't married yet, but they were saving money to get married. That was accepted in their culture. She came to me one night and asked if her mother asked about her to say she had been babysitting late at my place. I told her I hoped her mother didn't ask, as I would not lie for her. I had assumed she had wanted to spend some time with her boyfriend. How could her mother be upset, they had two children, she must know they were doing something sometime. Gloria said she had to go someplace tonight, it was important for her future. She had been asking for advances for several months, and I thought nothing of it. When I told her I couldn't give her another advance, she literally started crying and screaming her life was over. I was so glad the kids weren't home. It took me five minutes to calm her down. When she finally agreed to tell me what was wrong, it was only with the promise that I swore on a bible not to tell anyone, especially her mother or Mr. Tomaso, since he was such good friends with the Constable. Voodoo ceremonies are frowned upon and the law can consider money given for ceremonies bribery and a legal matter.

Apparently the father of her children's mother wanted him to marry and shopkeeper instead of a maid. She had put a curse on Gloria, and tonight was the ceremony to be rid of this spirit. Rather I believed it or not wasn't important, she did, and was terrified. I told her I didn't have any cash or I would give it to her. Please would I come with her and guarantee the money so that the sacrifice could be made? I looked at this poor woman, and realized she was trapped on this island, and would live here the rest of her life, with this belief system. She had no one to turn to, I had to help her.

I asked Julie to look after the kids when they came home from school, and left a note about some visiting. She asked me to take a white outfit in case they let me stay for the ceremony. The Priest owned a little shop so it wasn't unusual for us to be there. He was not pleased to see me with her. He asked Gloria to go outside while he talked with me.

"Isn't your husband the one that runs with the Constable?" he asked in a harsh voice. I knew where this was going. "That is true, but I'm here as Gloria's friend to see that she receives whatever it is she needs from you. I do not have any money tonight, but within two days I assure you I'll have the money for you. It will be my money, and my husband will know nothing about this" I said as I stared him right back. He asked me what I knew about Voodoo. I told him I knew nothing, except I heard people go into trances.

He decided to give me a little history lesson. It is a religion which was brought over from Africa with the slaves. Like your religion, we have two primary sorts; Rada is a family spirit of the peaceful and happy loa, and Petro is referred to as black magic of angry and mean loa, which could include death curses. Gloria has a curse put on her, and we are to have a ceremony to release these spirits from her. The Catholic goes to church to speak about God, and we have ceremonies with dances to become God. We believe the same as you in only one god, but we communicate with the divine through thousands of spirits, which we call Loa. The souls of the decreased act as intermediaries between God and the living. This relationship with the spirits is the essence of voodoo, we believe that the soul of the living has been momentarily displaced by the God, so that human being becomes the god. One of our main things we Priests do that you don't hear about is healing, telling the future, reading dreams, and casting spells to create protection. Do you have any questions you want to ask me?

In truth, I believe some of this, as probably my writing my name as Tomaso's wife 100 times could have been like a spell! I've studied hypnosis and know it works. It happens when you're in deep extension of concentration, in a state of deep relaxation, bypassing the critical factor of the conscious mind. You claim your complete attention, now using the power of suggestion. It's a 100% voluntary state, you cannot be forced to do something against your will as some people claim. It's practiced by medical doctors and university professors, and recognized as a science. We actually are in this natural state of mind each day without realizing it, a conscious relaxation. Self-hypnosis occurs when we become engrossed in something like reading, television, listening to music or driving our car. The Ancient Greeks and Romans used it for therapeutic benefit as far back at the fourth Century BC. I remember going to a workshop with my bridge partner and Katie's Nursing instructor on how hypnotism is now suggested as a healing method for many human problems. It can help people learn how to alleviate problems of public speaking or to stop smoking. Before anesthesia was discovered in 1853, Dr. James Esdaile of Edinburgh had used hypnosis on more than 2,000 patients during surgery. The human brain naturally produces a pain-relieving chemical compound called endorphin. So in truth, we are going backwards from a natural pain killer to paying the medical profession for help.

THE FINAL COMMANDMENTS

Every day we have been hypnotized by our parents and our surroundings sometimes leading to low self-esteem, depression, stress sexual identity and gender confusion. If you are being told as a child your are lazy and good for nothing, that is what you will believe, lacking self-confidence. It is believed that human beings have three types of mind. The conscious mind plays the analytical and judgmental role. The unconscious mind controls the automatic functions of the body and immune system, and holds temporary memory. The will power is a part of this and comes from life conditioning. Will power works in a strange way, the more you want to change something, like smoking, the more you fail. If I told you NOT to think of a blue elephant, what do you do? You think of the elephant! No, actually voodoo is not that far off from hypnosis. My mind came back to the present situation. "No, I have no other questions, I just want to make sure Gloria can have her ceremony tonight" I said.

"The money is for the sacrifice, so you will have to come to the ceremony and convince the gentlemen doing the sacrifice" he said with a sheepish grin. It was a challenge to my belief system. "If that's what it takes for Gloria, I will come." It was very unusual for them to let a stranger attend. I think he did it to get better control of the people. If anything bad happened to me, he could just say he put a curse on me for telling about the ceremony. We were all dressed in white. It was held outside under a thatched roof around the poto mitan center pole. Drums were used to provide the exciting beat that whipped people into a frenzy. The sacrifice was a chicken. There were several that were possessed that night, yet when it was over, they didn't remember it. Gloria knew nothing, but was informed by the voodoo priest the spirit was cast out. After that, Gloria seemed back to normal again.

We had met this unusual couple that had brought down 150 foot converted minesweeper. Lou Black was an electronic genius. He'd made a lot of money on some sort of navigational instrument. He'd just gone through a divorce, remarried, and had purchased his ship from the Coast Guard. His dry run for the Black Douglas was made in a movie. Rock Hudson was in a movie called "Operation Zebra" where they were tracking a Russian trawler. The Black Douglas had a Russian cycle painted on its side and was the Russian ship. When he returned to California for the final Coast Guard inspection, they told him he needed another $150,000 repairs to pass their inspection. At the time it was sold to him they'd said everything was okay. Another man at odds with the authority, no wonder he and Tomaso got along so well.

He took on a partner also. So in the dead of night, Lou, Pat his wife, and Al his partner took off for the Panama Canal. Pat had no idea what was happening. They put her down in the steerage and commanded her how to turn the ship! The three of them brought that 150-foot ship from California to Grand Turk by themselves. They bribed their way through the Panama, and made arrangements to fly the Turks and Caicos Flag for 40% of whatever treasure they found.

They were on their way to the United States to restock the ship at the same time we were leaving, so we sailed back with them to the states. It was a little dicey going through the cannel off of Cuba, as his giro was off. We came within Cuba's territory boundaries and were given a warning. We were lucky as they could have boarded us and did what they wished.

THE FINAL COMMANDMENTS

Before we left the island, we had one last unusual party. We used the ship as the setting and had small boats bring people out to the ship. There was a big fireworks display at the end of the evening.

I believe the Administrator was quite pleased to see the end of our unusual extravaganzas. He probably felt himself fortunate we hadn't blown the island up before we left.

4

FROM RICHES TO RAGS

Coming back to the United States, we realized we had missed five years of American culture. From 1965 to 1969, we weren't aware of TV programs, popular songs, styles, and inventions, what was important to the world.

We stayed in Wichita with my sister until Tomaso got the school set up. My sister took me to a grocery store where I ran up and down the frozen food aisles asking her to explain everything to me. Garage sales were a marvel! Everything we had on the island had been used, every piece of wire, pans, EVERYTHING.

Our next stop, in the middle of winter, was Colorado Springs for the instructor's pilot's license. The kids saw snow for the first time, which was a shock, perhaps, not altogether a pleasant one.

THE FINAL COMMANDMENTS

It was not a pleasant time for me either. We had given away nearly everything we had before leaving the island, and now, back in the states, I could see all the material things we didn't have, and I yearned for social contacts. Culture shock set in. In the islands, our social circle was an international mix of people and parties. In Colorado, I sat in a basement, in the snow, with no way to make social contact with anyone, just watching TV. It was one of the lowest times in my life.

I yearned to be learning something also, so I started taking flying lessons. This didn't last very long, but I got a taste of learning new things. I made up my mind at that time that I would always, in some way, be educating myself, no matter where I lived.

As we prepared to return to the island, Lou Black offered to let us live with him and his wife on the Black Douglas. They had bought a island so he could test his electrical equipment for the two-man submarine he was building for treasure hunting.

We ended up on an island seven miles away from everywhere, with absolutely nothing on it but prickly pears, a cactus fruit. Lou said he would school the older children, while Pat and I would take care of our babies. I would stay on the ship to bake bread and be in charge of the "shit line," while Tomaso and Al would build a dock and house.

We had been able to save a lot of money, as living overseas you don't pay taxes, living expenses were one fourth of living in the States, and there was no place to spend any money. A bottle of Jack Daniel's and a carton of cigarettes were $1.00 from the PX. In figuring the costs for the plane, Tomaso forgot to include insurance. We had enough money for the plane, but in three years the insurance would be the cost of the plane.

In a span of less than a year, I had spiraled downwards from living on the beach, children going to private school, playing bridge and on the list to the best parties, a maid and nanny, to living in a basement in the snow with no outside human social contact, to living on a converted minesweeper with three children being in charge of the shit-line. Every time I thought, "This is my life at its lowest point," my life just seemed to get a little worse.

On the Black Douglas, I felt I had no personal identity, toiling in survival mode for my family. Tomaso had spent most of the money we'd saved for five years on setting up this flying school. I felt like we were prisoners on the island because the only way off was by boat. Tomaso loved that type of life, as he didn't really like people.

I knew something had to change, but didn't know how to go about it. Looking back, I can see, working in my life even then, without knowing it, the Law of Dharmic direction: listen to your inner direction, your inner guiding principle. Rather people realize it or not, every thought is a type of prayer or mediation. There are several ladder of prayer. The lowest thought pattern is worry, and doesn't help you any. Next is the unconsciousness call for help (there must be a better way) which was the level I was at, and then a conscious call for help.

I truly believe the universe helps you when you ask for guidance. There was literally no way for us to get off the island, as the men were the only ones that left to get electrical supplies. We had stores of canned goods and flour for six months. One night Katie ran a very high fever. The weather was stormy and we had to get her to the main island. First we had to get her on the tram that went to the ship. It was horrible, with the wind and rain blowing. Then we had to get her in a small boat that was bobbing violently up and down with the waves. We had a slow, soggy, crazy trip to the main island of Grand Turk.

Katie lay in the hospital for five days. I kept promising her we wouldn't go back to the ship; I would take her away from these islands. I went to the next ladder of prayer, which is the petition for things (give me this and I'll never ask again or I'll change my ways).

Tomaso was off on another island doing a project for the Turks & Caicos Government. We had a few bonds in the bank. I went to the bank, got the bonds, purchased four tickets to Hawaii, and the day Katie got out of the hospital, I took the kids to the airport and headed for Hawaii.

This was a very traumatic time for us. Again, we left all our belongings behind, and took just what would fit in suitcases. I had been away for over five years. I got a position easily enough with my previous work experience, but was shocked to see how much prices had increased. I couldn't find a place to live with three children. For the first time, I really could not take care of my children. I was scared. It was a sobering moment. Finally, in despair, I called their father to ask if they could live with him and go to school until I could save up some money. If ever there were guardian angels in my life, it was William and his wife. How many women would lovingly welcome another woman's children into her home in a moment's notice?

I swore from that moment forward, I wouldn't let myself get in that predicament again. Education was going to be at the top of my priority list so I wouldn't have to rely on anyone.

I started saving my money, spending only on absolute necessities. Tomaso wrote and wanted to come to Hawaii. By this time, the only thing between us was our son. He accused, "You can go any place any time you want. But you don't take my son. He is all I have to live for."

I could feel the pain in his voice. I didn't know what to do. My other children were 1,500 miles away, I had a minimal job, and he had no job. I charged a plane ticket for him.

Soon, he was offered a position on the island of Kauai, a hundred miles away. If I went with him, I'd be able to bring my children back.

Living on Kauai was completely different than Oahu. The island closed at sundown; no stores or gas stations were open. We found an old house to rent in Poipu, only one block from the beach, which was a good place for the children.

I found a job working weekends scheduling helicopter rides. Jordan got a paper route and we got him a bike. Tomaso drove a long way to and from work, so we rarely saw each other. I eventually got a second full time job, and continued working both of them as long as I could. I wanted money in the bank so I would never again be in the position of being unable to take care of my family, or under another person's control.

Tomaso eventually left again, to Johnston Island in the Pacific. I had been promised a raise at my main job. When I reminded the company president, he said he couldn't give me a raise because I would be making more money than one of the long-term employees. I reminded him that what I was making was not what was agreed upon. He kept his word and gave me the raise. The other employee was extremely angry and quit. I told him I would take on her duties if he'd let me take an accounting course at the Community College. My love affair with knowledge began. My desire for travel had been replaced with knowledge. Married in Las Vegas, divorced in Los Angeles; married in Florida, lived in British West Indies, and divorced in Hawaii. I was ready for some stability.

When Tomaso left, financial hardship threatened again, but the company coworkers treated me as family. I will never forget that feeling, knowing that I was one of the family. The company president said he couldn't give me any more raises, but he could help in other ways. He fixed up a company owned home for me to rent at a very reasonable price, which was closer to work. He arranged an additional job with a contractor's association.

Finally I found a social life. I joined a sorority, a professional woman's club, and found time for bridge. It felt wonderful to be around intellectual people again. I filed for divorce, asking for no financial assistance, and received legal custody of Michael.

In only months, Tomaso started pressuring for more visitations with his son. I considered how much he loved Michael and their strong emotional bond. Financially, money was extremely tight. I knew Tomaso could provide a living, so I agreed to let him take Michael, with the understanding that he had to remain in the United States. I would maintain legal custody. This would give me a chance to get my accounting degree and a better income.

Katie and Jordan had gone back to spend the summer with their father. With all the children gone, the house was too lonely and quiet. Night classes were a relief.

One evening after our women's club meeting, some friends and I stopped by the local restaurant for dinner and drinks. We ended up at the Golden Cape, a beautiful club at the top of the highest hotel on Kauai, with a beautiful view of the bay.

It felt good not to be studying, but laughing and being around other people.

A deep voice whispered in my ear, "I can see why there would be angels in here, it's so close to heaven."

My friend Shirley and I both turned at the same time to see a handsome Hawaiian Japanese man dressed in a beautiful silk shirt, navy blue pants, and very expensive shoes. His eyes were piercing, and his smile said, "I always get what I want."

Shirley laughed and said, "Kenji, what are you doing in from the west side, looking for new tourists?"

He touched my elbow and electricity shot through me. "No, tonight I want to meet this angel you have with you."

Shirley introduced us and we danced all night, with very little conversation. It had been so long since I had actually felt anything, I just kept dancing. I felt so alive, laughing and dancing.

We closed the Golden Cape, and he asked me if I wanted to come to his room. I knew somehow the decision I made tonight would affect me for years to come. I declined, so we went for saimin and made a date for dinner the next night. He asked me what my favorite food was, and I told him lobster, which wasn't available on Kauai.

He said, "You'll have lobster tomorrow night."

The next day two dozen roses were delivered, confirming the time and place we were to meet. When he picked me up, we drove out to the airport. Next thing I knew, we were on a plane to Honolulu. We had lobster in the tallest hotel in Honolulu. When we finished dinner, it was too late to fly back to Kauai, 9 P.M was the latest flight.

THE FINAL COMMANDMENTS

Looking at me with those piercing eyes, he said, "You must know by now I take care of all the details, so you will have everything you need to stay overnight. I can get one room or two, it's up to you."

I knew I wouldn't just be walking away from him. I liked the idea of someone else taking care of details, of not having to worry about anything for twenty-four hours. Time to laugh, make love, and enjoy life. No small talk, any responsibilities. It was another universal law at work, the Law of dominant desire: the stronger emotion will dominate the weaker one. At that moment in my life, what he offered is just what I wanted.

Shirley filled me in on him. He was married, but went down-town every weekend looking for tourist. She warned me not to get involved and get hurt. He was a man with no feelings.

On a small island, just like in a small community, people know everything about everybody. My boss, Mr. Hamada, called me in one day and mentioned word had come to him that I'd been seen at the Golden Cape with Kenji, and Moki Williams, who was connected to the Hawaiian Mafia and it wasn't safe to be with these people. Some people having deal-ings with them had just disappeared. I remembered now that we would borrow Moki's car when we went to Honolulu.

One evening I was working at a contractor's meeting where the guest speaker was Chief of Police Ray Hee. He was Hawaiian Chinese and just returned after many years with the San Jose Police Department in California. After the meeting Chief Hee came over and spoke with me. He invited me to lunch. Over the meal, he asked about my goals and ambitions. We discussed California, and how hard it was to fit in on Kauai.

"Why do you waste your time at Night College?" he abruptly asked. "With all your connections, I'd think you could make good money?" I looked at him, puzzled.

He said, "I thought you were keeping the books for Kenji's business too." I didn't remember mentioning Kenji at all. When I looked up from my salad, I could see he had been staring at me through the whole conversation. I knew something was wrong, but I didn't know what it was.

One night when I came home from school, Ray called and made me an offer I couldn't refuse, a picnic overlooking the most beautiful spot on the island.

When I arrived, a beautiful spread was arranged on the tablecloth. Pupu's and a virgin Mai Tai were waiting. I was impressed. I could tell he had a kind heart and a tender soul.

He said very quietly, "The police department has been investigating you for an undercover operation regarding Kenji. I had to be sure you weren't involved. Someone asked us, off the record, to make sure you are not involved or hurt by these people."

I knew that must have been Mr. Hamada, but I had no idea what he was talking about.

He asked how much I knew about Moki Williams, who was suspected of being involved in drug smuggling. Kenji was also under suspicion. I told him I had only met Moki Williams once, and then got angry. I liked Kenji and felt like I was betraying him, and I felt like Ray wanted me to be a spy.

I started to leave, but he took my hand. "This will never be mentioned again. I will make sure that you are protected. I've been studying you for months. I like your character, and I'm happy you're not involved. Otherwise, I wouldn't be able to do this."

THE FINAL COMMANDMENTS

He took his hand and turned my face toward him, brushing back my hair. It was a gentle kiss, our lips barely touching. Time seemed to be frozen. He laid his head on my chest, and we both fell asleep.

I was torn between my weekends with Kenji and my evenings with Ray. Neither was a secure relationship.

Katie would be returning in a few weeks. Their father called, asking if Jordan could stay. He had been on a Pop Warner football team and wanted to stay with the group. I agreed that if this is what he wanted, and they felt was best, I wouldn't stand in the way.

Now it would be just Katie and me. I knew some decisions had to be made. I had to give her a better home. I knew the beautiful home she had been visiting and felt guilty not to be able to offer her better. Everything fell in place to help me with my decisions.

Mr. Hamada had mentioned to me again about the danger of the company I was keeping. Kenji had gotten wind of me seeing Ray and was really mad. I reminded him he went home to his wife during the week. He was furious, but so was I. I was tired of people telling me what to do.

Katie came back, but after a couple of weeks, I received a call from her father. She had called him about how lonely she was. I felt so bad. I quit night school and started looking for another job so we could get a better home. Then Kenji came with house plans. He was getting a divorce, he said, and we could build our own home. I didn't know if he was doing this just so I wouldn't see Ray or if he was serious.

One day he took me for a drive to the top of a large mountain near a beautiful waterfall. A judge who was a friend of mine pulled in next to us. We followed them to a lot he owed two blocks away. He wanted to know if the location was good for me. I said yes, and we drove back to their home where Kenji paid cash for the lot. I guess he was serious. It just seemed like everything was decided for me.

He had just sold his tourist business, so I went to work over there. I wouldn't go while he owned it. I thought that would be too much control over me. The three of us made our house plans, ordered our furniture, and watched the home go up. Now Katie would have a nice home too. Also, this was the first home I had ever owned. I told him I wanted to pay my share. He said I didn't have to worry, the house would be under both our names, with joint survivorship. I insisted we go to an attorney to record a loan for half the land to be paid off in eight years. I didn't have to do that, but I wanted to know myself that I was paying half. Kenji was always fair with me.

Ray called, and I told him I wouldn't be able to see him. He said he understood, but needed to see me to tell me something. I agreed to meet him.

"This is not the path I would have chosen for you, but it is the one you have chosen. Did you know that Don Ho and I used to go to school together at Kamehameha?" he asked. "I saw him on my last trip to Honolulu and we ended up talking about the haole that got away! I'm bringing this up, as I don't think you are aware of how spiritual Hawaiians are. Shamans have guided the Hawaiian people for hundreds of years. They guide us and ask us to help when certain people have a destiny to fulfill. Don saw this in you many years ago."

I laughed and said, "Now you want me to help you fulfill your destiny?"

THE FINAL COMMANDMENTS

"It's not you helping us," he answered, "but us helping you. I know what I'm going to say isn't going to make sense to you now, but one day it will," he said as he held my arm to keep me from leaving, and looked me straight in the eye to let me know how serious this was.

This was too much for me. Was he trying to get even with me for building a home with Kenji? Everyone was trying to tell me what to do. Kenji said he didn't want me going to college at night to come home to an empty home, Mr. Hamada didn't want me seeing certain people, and now Ray wanted me to go on some spiritual trip. I told Ray all I wanted was a nice home for my daughter, and no one telling me how to live my life. I knew right then I would never marry again, no one would ever have control over me again.

He released the hold he had on my arm, and took my hand gently. "Natasha, look at me." I looked up and saw such pain in his eyes. "I have seen part of your destiny. You do have a mission in life, and any time you need help, you can call on us. When you get a chance, I want you to study with a Shaman. When the time is right, you'll choose the right one. You have many, many years of learning ahead, and most of it won't be in comfort. Just remember, as long as you are learning, you are fulfilling your destiny."

I could think of nothing to say, what is there to say to someone who has just told you there is a mission in life for you and it won't be pleasant? I said goodbye, and when I turned to leave, he took my hand and said the strangest goodbye. "Peace is your mission."

I didn't want any secrets between us, so I told Kenji I had lunch with Ray. He laughed and said, "I know. He must have really been drunk to say all those things. I wish I'd realized earlier he was no threat to me."

What a strange thing to say, I thought. Apparently he had someone at the restaurant listening to our conversation.

Things went well for a few years. We took trips to Japan and Europe. I thought nothing of his trips to Honolulu, as he always had business there.

In fairness to Kenji, I took many trips by myself. I spent three months in Asia on a summer abroad with University of Hawaii. I attended the International Year of the Woman Conference in Mexico City as a delegate for the United Nations.

Then one day I was at the airport to pick something up, I saw Kenji taking another woman to Honolulu. For the first time, I knew the pain of being cheated on. I thought of how many women I knew who tried to hang on to something lost. I had already determined years before emotions would not rule my life. His cheating hurt me, but the thought of losing the house hurt more. It was the only home I had ever had.

I told him this behavior was unacceptable to me. My concern was for Katie, and for giving her a proper home.

We both went our own way, just sharing the house. I started thinking of ways to buy his half of the house.

I worked four jobs, trying to get enough money to purchase the house. I worked as night auditor at the Holiday Inn, then half a day as field director at the American Red Cross, was appointed to the tax commission by then Governor George Ariyoshi, and kept a set of books for a restaurant.

Oprah says the Universe will give you a small nudge, then a bigger one, and if you don't move in the right direction, a brick will fall on you.

THE FINAL COMMANDMENTS

In the middle of all of this, a medical exam showed that I had cervical cancer. My mother had died from the same cancer at the same age I was then. I remember my mother suffered so much from new experiments the doctors tried on her. They burned her inside with radium capsules, and when she couldn't stand the pain, they cut nerve muscles, which also meant she couldn't walk. At that time people just assumed the doctor was always right and knew the right procedures. I was not going to let anyone make these decisions for me.

I started reading everything I could get my hands on, and remembered Ray's suggestion of a Shaman. A shaman was not only a spiritual guide but also was a tribal healer. I started growing wheat grass and changed my eating habits. I choose the method for the doctors, and it didn't include some cutting they wanted to do. Through my research, I also took stock of my life. I realize now that karma was at work then, in that the Law of Conscious Detachment, resistance causes pain.

The Universe was telling me it was time to let go of that house, and go on with my life. The house was holding me back. This was the first step for me to let go of material things. Katie was grown and in nursing school. Keeping the house would mean working three or four jobs and renting out a room to make ends meet. It was time to move on. The house was put up for sale, and I got my portion in cash.

When Katie graduated, I left home. I applied to the University of Hawaii, and received a two-year grant to finish my Business Administration degree. I still had problems getting rid of everything. I packed boxes and left some with Kenji and some with Ray to store for me. The Law of Release says to let go of anything that's not useful without regret. Free yourself for a new experience.

I took a trip to Fuji, Australia, and Samoa in the month before school started. I was drawn to Ayres Rock in the center of Australia, and at the time couldn't figure out why. Now I realize it is one of the most holistic places on this earth, a very spiritual place. At that point in my life I had no idea what the word spiritual meant. I had beaten cancer, so I knew every moment of my life from then on was going to be exciting. The self-fulfilling prophecy of dying the same death and at the same age of my mother was over. I was beginning to understand the power of the mind, of will. It was the Law of Manifestation: what begins as a thought creates your reality.

5

TRAVEL AROUND THE WORLD

This was truly a new chapter in my life. The Law of New Beginnings, major life changing times has break in brain pattern. I was ready to live life to the fullest, and fulfill my dream of a proper education. I was going to stay on campus in their apartment complex. You had four students to an apartment, two to a room. I was 43 years old, I could have been the mother of any of these students. Now I realize that there are no accidents, you are put together with people for one reason or another. The Law of Association, two or more has a commonality it can influence the outcome.

We were perfectly matched, or mismatched would be more correct. The brain was a Astrology major; I couldn't have passed calculus without her help. The second one was majoring in Nutrition, which was about her fifth major. She'd been in several different Universities for almost ten years so she wouldn't have to pay back her student loans. It would be a toss up of which one was the most indecisive, as the third was in Library School, trying to decide if this was the correct major.

The University has 27,000 students, the same amount of people living on Kauai. It was so stimulating, there was a lecture or some intellectual function all the time. Having to study and being in classes didn't give me much time to consider the changes in my life. We did manage to walk down to the Rhino Bar, a watering hole for the students. It was like the years I missed after high school, only I was 25 years older. I didn't enjoy the tests and studying, but I did enjoy the knowledge there for the taking.

Living in Hawaii I was use to the culture of Asia and Polynesia. Now I was meeting students from Pakistan and Africa, two very diverse cultures, with there own agenda for their nations. One of my bridge partners was from Pakistan, and a very happy individual. He was completing is Ph.D. in Chemistry. He was from a small village in the country, and his marriage was arranged with a beautiful woman that was raised in England of a higher class. They were Moslem, and she had no choice in the matter. This was fine on this beautiful island in Hawaii, but what would her life be when she moved to this little dirt village he was from. I shutter to think of the fate of some women, even in this day and age. This was the first time I had met a Moslem, and had no idea how much their culture would figure in my life later on.

The other new person in my life was an angry man from Zimbabwe, although it might be called something else now. He was still angry at the whites for taking over his country years ago. I thought of Tomaso and how they had gone down and purchased the best land, and had the natives as workers. I certainly wasn't going to mention this to him, he was angry enough.

Since my cancer scare, I made sure that every moment of my life was lived to the fullest. "Life should NOT be a journey to the grave with the intention of arriving safely in an attractive and well preserved body, but rather to skid in sideways, throttle in one hand – clutch in the other, body thoroughly use up, totally worn out and screaming WOO HOO – What a Ride!" – Indian Larry This was my exact thoughts about life. I went dancing on the weekends at the Top of the Iliki, the most beautiful view in Honolulu. There was nothing spiritual about my life, it was all about living with gusto. However, I was getting education, and that was my main goal now. Time passed, and soon it was time for graduation. I had to think about graduate school, and was going for the MBA. Then came Law of Darmic Direction, an inside guiding principle. There were several relationships and circumstances that changed my decision. One of my coworkers had lived in Egypt. I hadn't paid too much attention to the fact until I was looking for a place to do some Graduate courses. I had decided to take a semester off and do a trip around the world. I would spend part of the time taking graduate classes. She had worked at the American University of Cairo, and even married an Egyptian. Since the credits could be transferred easily, I had decided to spend a summer semester there.

The other thing was the use of computers. Right now I had to get up at 2 A.M. to get on the mainframe. Another employee was also in Library School. She told me they had their own computers in the basement of the library where their school was. I went over and spoke to the Dean regarding the program.

It appears that information science was just becoming very important. Although it was a Library Degree, many companies were now hiring Librarians just to handle their information systems. Besides the computer room, they had nap rooms, a kitchen, and great private study areas. There was only 100 hundred students enrolled in the program. It wouldn't be like the business courses where you're graded on a curve, and in lecture rooms of fifty or more students. The idea of having your own computer space was too much to resist.

Some people could call this just a coincidence. I have come to learn that there is a natural order to things. The Law of Divine order, no accidents, your energy, translated in thoughts and feelings, cause all your experiences. What I needed at that time in my life was provided for me. I needed certain information to make a decision. I had decided on Graduate work in Library and Information Science when I returned. I would go to summer session in Egypt.

One of my bridge partners was going to England, Scandinavia, Russia, Poland, Germany, and the Netherlands. She was a Psychiatrist and would make a great traveling companion. Although I had already been to Europe, these were not places we had visited. I told her I would go with her, meet her in England, then catch my around the world ticket in Europe and continue. I would have to leave the tour earlier to be in Egypt for the summer semester.

Russia was the most interesting. I can see now why the people revolted. The Hermitage Museum, which used to be the summer palace, was magnificent. The bathroom facets were made of gold, while the people were starving. The people in the villages were very friendly, wanting to trade little trinkets.

THE FINAL COMMANDMENTS

I ended the trip early going through East Germany by train, where I was woken in the middle of the night to check my passport. The Berlin wall was still up at this time. When I arrived in the Netherlands, I took a plane to Greece.

Flying from Athens to Egypt was an exciting experience. I could hardly wait to see the Pyramids for the first time. I always think of the song that was popular when I graduated from High School. It started, "See the Pyramids along the Nile". At that time I would have never imagined I would ever see them. I remember how I envied one of my classmates who went to Hawaii on vacation. I just couldn't imagine someone having the money to travel that far, it wasn't a State at that time. This shows the limit of my imagination at that point of my life. Years later I would be living in Hawaii, showing her the treasures of my island and having her and her husband over for dinner while on vacation.

I made sure I sat on the right side to see the Pyramids and waited for hours staring at the dry barren desert. Finally I saw lights in the distance, miles and miles of lights. I kept searching, my eyes looking at every square afraid I would miss them. Finally, there stood three pyramids, casting their grandeur to the sky. To this date, that sight is the greatest inspiration I have ever had. I could hear the wind whispering through the sands, "You simple mortals, I have been here for thousands of years, the oldest man made structure in the world, and you still will not believe how I was built. Everything you need to know is inside you, and right inside me, but you choose to argue over unimportant things, instead of discovering the truth about the universe and living in harmony."

The lady next to me asked me where I was going to stay. We wouldn't be arriving until 2 A.M. so I told her I'd just wait in the airport till morning. She gave out a loud laugh that made everyone turn and stare.

"You silly girl, you're in Egypt now. You don't just hang around the airport. First, there's no place to sit, and there will be tourist police wanting to know what you're doing. You could end up in jail without a place to stay."

As we cleared customs I learned what she was talking about. They made me show proof that I had enough cash money for a month, a return ticket, and an address. When the month's worth of money ran out, the visa had to be renewed or go to jail.

The woman knew I was a student, so she actually took me to a Hotel in downtown Cairo. It was more like a Pension, where Professors on a dig or doing on a research project would stay. I would have never found this place on my own. There was a tiny sign that read 'Pension on the third floor.' She yelled harshly in Arabic and right away there was a reply " Iywa, iywa". We could hear a man's steps hurrying down the stairs.

She found out the bawwab's name was Mohammed; each building has a doorman that guards the building with his life. Mohammed couldn't have weighed more than 90 pounds, and must have been 100 years old! She spoke very fast and loudly to Mohammed and he kept saying, " Iywa, iywa" as he started to drag my heavy suitcase up the stairs.

I asked, "Isn't the elevator working?"

She belly laughed again. " You are in Egypt, you'll soon find out that nothing works."

She told Mohammed to "protect" me and see that I got to Zamalek and the Hostel tomorrow. "Don't pay the clerk more than five Egyptian pounds. Tell him you know how much it costs and you'll turn him in. Let Mohammed take care of the suitcases, you can trust him. Don't try to help him, it will be an insult to him. Just take the one suitcase you need to your room. Mohammed will guard the others all night. Mohammed will get you a taxi in the morning, and negotiate the ride for fifty piasters. You can tip Mohammed tomorrow one Egyptian pound, not more. Trust Mohammed, not the clerk. He will tell you the phone isn't working, which will probably be true. The clerk will try to extort money for sending someone with a message. Just ignore him. If Mohammed thinks the taxi driver isn't reliable, he will go with you. Then you can tip him another pound. He can walk back or you can give the taxi driver another fifty piasters for his return."

She took my hand softly and held it. I actually looked at her for the first time. She had beautiful dark eyes, and I saw a real tenderness in her face.

"I could tell by the way you looked at the Pyramids that you are one of the chosen. You will be living in Egypt and become one of the seekers of the truth. There will be many, many trips to the land of the Pharaohs. In the years to come, the world will become worse, not better. Each one of us will have to do whatever is needed to bring order to our world."

I though it was a strange thing to say to someone you had just met. I explained I was only here for the summer session, not really living here.

She gave her great belly laugh again. "There is a saying in Egypt. When you drink from the Nile, you will return. Believe me, you will be back. Ma'salamah."

She turned and disappeared. It was at this moment I remembered we hadn't even exchanged names. Here I was standing in the middle of the night, no one on the streets, in an area that looked like the slums, with two oversized suitcases, and one being dragged up three flights of stairs. I didn't speak a word of Arabic, and was entrusted to Mohammed, whom I couldn't communicate with.

Mohammed came back down speaking Arabic and smiling, waving me with his hands up the stairs. Somehow I did trust this kind soul, and followed him up three flights of stairs. He led me to a room, showed me where the bathroom was, and said ' Ma'salamah' as he shut the door. I was so tired I couldn't think of anything but sleep. I didn't even take my cloths off. I just pulled the sheet over me.

I woke up to the first call to prayer at sunrise. There was a minuet just a few yards from the Pension. I found out later that this isn't unusual, as Cairo is known as the city of 1,000 mosques, more than any place else in the world. It was a beautiful sound, like a song being sung.

My next encounter wasn't as pleasant. I heard several voices loudly arguing down the hall. I recognized Mohammed as one. I heard my name several times, and wondered how they knew it since I hadn't registered. Then I remembered my nametag on the suitcases. I quickly straightened my hair and went towards the voices. There were two policemen, a very dark unpleasant man, and Mohammed. When they saw me, all conversation stopped. One of the policemen headed for me, pointing his gun at me and yelling in Arabic. The dark unpleasant man started yelling at him and stood between us.

"He is upset because you didn't register last night, and gave the wrong address of where you were going."

I tried to explain the Hostel wouldn't be open till 9:00 A.M. and when I left the airport I didn't know where I was going. When I couldn't answer the question of what the lady's name was that brought me her, or where she went, I felt foolish.

After thirty minutes of yelling at each other it came down to this. Mohammed had been given strict instructions not to wake the clerk. The clerk of course didn't mean if there was a guest. There are laws in Egypt that foreigners must obey. The Egyptian Government has the right to know where foreigners are. I had broken that law. Unless the clerk got fifty pounds to straighten this out, Mohammed and perhaps myself would go to jail. He had a cousin that could help us out. I remembered what the lady had said about not trusting the clerk, but I couldn't talk to anyone but him. No one spoke English but the clerk. I could probably get myself out through the American Embassy, but I couldn't let Mohammed get in any trouble. I looked over to Mohammed for guidance. He kept shaking his head no.

"Quickly, make a decision and give me some money, or they'll take Mohammed away!" Just as I was about to go to my room to get the money, I heard the elevator start up.

The clerk was very anxious. He yelled at me, "Quickly, the Pasha is here, sign the register. Give me your passport!"

I was signing the register when I heard the elevator door shut. " Sabah el-kheir Pasha Aziz." After several greetings of everyone to each other, the clerk, the police, Mohammed, a soft-spoken gentlemen said, "and who is this Mademoiselle?"

"This is Madam Natasha Niska from America." Aziz replied, "and what are the police doing here?"

The clerk started to speak in Arabic, and Aziz corrected him, stating we had a guest and it was impolite not to speak in English. The clerk's face flushed red. He explained his cousin had sent a message to him that's all. "Since they have been here over one hour, I guess you have your message by now." He explained they were just having tea and was ready to leave.

Aziz turned to me and said, "I hope it didn't overcharge you last night, it was five pounds wasn't it?"

"Yes, of course, Pasha Aziz, it was only five pounds."

"Good, hand me the five pounds and I'll take it to the bank." I started to say something about not giving him the money yet and the clerk quickly handed him five pounds.

Aziz turned to me and said, "I imagine you are in a hurry to get to the hostel. My car is downstairs, I'll drive you over there." He turned and started giving instructions to Mohammed, who quickly started dragging my suitcases to the elevator. When I came out of the room the clerk had his back to me, looked very busy. I went down in the elevator with Aziz. He saw my bewilderment, and before I could say anything said, "I have a key to the elevator."

There was an immaculate black Mercedes with a driver sitting in front of the building. He looked at my amazement and started laughing.

"Are you amazed at the car, the driver, or finding a parking spot?" He explained there are people whose job is to push cars back and forth and make parking spots. When I had arrived late at night the cars were parked two deep, and I had wondered how they got their cars out.

THE FINAL COMMANDMENTS

I had been in a city of thirteen million for less than ten hours and the police knew where I was, and a complete stranger that owned the hotel that I stayed at was aware of what I was doing in Cairo. I had discovered the one to trust was the lowest of the servants. This was going to be an amazing place.

"We are supposed to serve you breakfast at the Pension, but you didn't eat. May I take you to breakfast before I drive you to the Hostel?" The Marriott Hotel was only two blocks from the Hostel, so we had breakfast there. It used to be one of King Farouk's palaces and is right on the Nile. What a wonderful introduction to Egypt. Aziz asked me if he might call on me in a few days when I got settled to show me the Pyramids.

Aziz's driver couldn't take the bags up, as this was an all girls' residence. He had to leave them downstairs. The Director came down and arranged for their bawwab to get my bags.

"Who do you know in Cairo?" I explained that was Pasha Aziz.

She replied curtly, "There are no Pashas in Egypt since King Farouk. Trust no one that drives a Mercedes."

Living at the Hostel was an exhilarating experience. Most of the students were Americans, as they had a special Arabic program. So many girls stayed at the hostel that led such exciting lives! For me, it was a first encounter with women who actually planned their lives. One girl, Marianne, was beautiful, tall, slim, blue eyes and long blonde hair. She was in the Arabic study program and definitely there to experience the culture. Her boyfriends ranged from the stable boy to sheiks. She loved riding, and many Saudis kept horses in Egypt. Eventually, she ended up being a writer in the Middle East. We corresponded for years, but I lost track of her after Iraq invaded Kuwait, as she was living in Kuwait at the time. Helen was least like me. She was exceptionally quiet, dressed plainly, and always studying. If our mutual interest hadn't been computers, we wouldn't have had anything to talk about. Our paths would keep crossing through the rest of our lives.

Very quickly we learned about Egyptian cultural differences through dating Egyptian men. The Egyptian cultural expectations for male-female relationships are very complicated and difficult to understand. Egyptians can't date American style. They literally have to be engaged to hold hands. Morals police wandered around, checking to see that couples were not engaging in any improper behavior. Anything more than handholding implied ownership. In Egypt at that time, women were considered property. Marianne got involved with someone who was going to beat her up for her seeing another man and had to run to the American Embassy for protection.

Aziz called me and took me to the Pyramids. All the pictures and information I had read about them couldn't prepare me for the real thing. I went over all the facts I read about the Pyramids of Giza. The pyramids were the largest structures ever built until the Eiffel Tower. The oldest pyramid dated from between 2680 to 2565 BC according to Egyptians.

When I actually got to the base of the Pyramid and truly touched the stones, it was electrifying. I could only stand there in wonderment and try to imagine how these were built and by whom. For the first time, I felt connected to the universe and to everyone in it. I was aware of the connection of myself, as a human being, to people all over the world. I thought, "There must be some purpose to my life after all."

THE FINAL COMMANDMENTS

Actually, there is a Universal Law that encompasses that feeling. The Law of Psychometric Influences says people are affected by objects; physical contact influences mental connections.

I was pulled back to reality by the tour director of a group of people spouting facts and figures. "The measurements of the pyramid equal one solar year, the time it takes our earth to whirl around its center. It's referred to as a map of the universe. There are no hieroglyphics or writings in the Great Pyramid. Nova and the A.R.E. Edgar Cayce Foundation believe it to date back 10,500 years. It is estimated to contain 2,300,000 stones from 2 to 30 tons each, some weighing 70 tons. It covers an area of 13.6 acres, with each side equal to five acres in area. The stones have been placed to 5/1000ths of an inch, the most accurately aligned structure to true north. It is solid except for two chambers; the King's Chamber is approximately 46 feet long by 16 feet wide, and the Queen's Chamber is approximately 25 feet by 35 feet."

The group moved on as the tour guide kept giving more information. I asked Aziz, "Did I hear him right, the Pyramids are over 10,000 years old?"

He started laughing and said, "Oh that's just some group they call New Age, whatever that means. They're questioning everything about the Pyramid, making up their own facts about it."

He gave the guard baksheesh and got us inside the pyramid. Again this eerie feeling came over me and a chill ran up my spine. There was a small path with steep steps leading steeply upward at a sharp angle. Hanging on to a rope was the only way to keep from falling. Every few yards light bulbs pierced the darkness. We stood in the King and Queen Chambers without a word. What was there to say in the presence of this history?

I had so many questions about the Pyramids. I turned to Aziz for answers. How could it have been a burial chamber when there was no hieroglyphics? It was as large as five square blocks, solid except for the two small chambers. Burial chambers had room for all the treasures they take with them to the next life. How could masses of people drag those stones that even with today's technology we can't lift? How could their measurements be so accurate to the calendar and solar system?

"Mesh mumkenl!" he yelled. This meant impossible, leave it alone.

He gave me a stern look and just said, "Don't you be one of those crazy new age people who try to come over and change our history!"

He continued, "Our Director General of Giza, Dr. Zahi Hawass, knows the truth. He's studied this all his life, and is Egyptian. We do not need outsiders telling us about the Pyramids." That was the end of that. This strained our relationship, not even being able to discuss an idea. I didn't realize that in fifteen years I would be at a conference with the Edgar Cayce Foundation and Dr. Zahi Hawass would be one of the guest speakers.

I was shopping in Zamalek one day and couldn't figure out the price of something. I heard a voice behind me say softly, "Excuse me, but may I help you?" I turned to see the most attractive man I'd ever seen.

Seif and I had an intense romance, which contained all the passion and fire of a romance novel, except under the watchful eyes of the Egyptian morals police. We spent many afternoons in the courtyard of the hostel with Helen and Ahmed, and would go to the Sheraton for dinner. I was dating by my American upbringing; he was dating by the rules of his Egyptian culture, and eventually, they clashed. He had, by my actions, made the natural assumption from his culture that I would marry him, while I had assumed we were "just dating." I had to repeatedly explain my education goals to Seif, and finally I insisted that our relationship could not continue. In part, I felt good about that because I had made the decision. I couldn't remember the last time I had been in control.

Seif realized that I had plans that I couldn't change. He didn't know why I needed all this education but would honor it.

Seif continually asked when I would come back, until I agreed to come back during Christmas break. "Which Christmas?" he asked.

I didn't quite understand what he was talking about. Then he explained they had three Christmas dates in Egypt. There was the Coptic, the Greek, and the Christian. Later on in my studies I would learn that the church altered many of the dates in the Bible. Even the Sabbath was really on Saturday and was changed to Sunday.

Our parting was really hard, as I hadn't had deep emotions for many years. My goal was just to finish my next degree, and worry about the rest of my life after that. Egypt was 17,000 miles from Hawaii. Then I remembered the lady who took me to the Pension. She had said, "You will return several times, and live in Egypt." At this stage in my life, I couldn't imagine that as my course in life.

The rest of my trip included Israel where I stayed in a Kibbutz, and in the walled city of Jerusalem, where so much history lived, as in Egypt. The three major religious groups, Christian, Moslem, and Jewish had sites within shouting distance of each other. Later I would read the book 'Oh Jerusalem' that would really tear at my heart. The Moslems and Jews had lived side by side for centuries as neighbors, sharing each other's celebrations and family traditions, showing that it can be done. Then politics and religion moved in and the hate began.

I went by ship to Cypress, then to Greece. From Greece I took a tour to Turkey, which really put me at a disadvantage. I didn't speak Greek, Turkish, or Arabic. I flew to Sri Lanka, then to India where I stayed in an Ashram.

I wasn't really spiritually ready for this. Yoga was a daily practice. I thought it was just exercise. After my first encounter I could hardly walk. When I went to the first meal there were round pans on the floor. I thought they were for the dogs. We sat on the concrete floors and ate.

India was the only country that I didn't feel safe in, especially after coming from Egypt. In Egypt I would have walked the streets by myself at anytime. In India, the extreme poverty led to rampant crime. When they stole it wasn't for a pair of fancy Nike shoes, it was to feed their family. Gangs boarded the trains to steal. Hotel windows were barred.

I did go to the Buddha Tree, and imagined him setting there in silence. There is just something special about being in the same spot a great person occupied.

I flew to Katmandu in Nepal from India. This would be the closest I would get to Tibet, which would be figuring into my studies later on.

I must have caught some sort of bug in India. By the time I got on the plane to Hawaii perspiration was running down my body. I was afraid they weren't going to let me on the plane. Katie was living in Honolulu now doing her Business Degree. She had an apartment with my old roommate, the mathematician. I stayed with her for a few days until I could get in my campus housing.

It was a great greeting back in Hawaii. I had to go to the doctor, and wasn't allowed to fly back to Kauai to vote. I was down for about a week. Then there was a hurricane Iwa on Thanksgiving Day. Kauai, our island, got the brunt of it. Honolulu received some damage, with electricity being off for a few days.

6

UNIVERSITY OF HAWAII
GRADUATE SCHOOL

The atmosphere for Graduate Library School was a 360 degree turn. There were only 100 of us enrolled at one time. We had our own key to the school, which was housed in the basement of Hamilton Library. Our computers were provided, plus a real atmosphere to study. Large tables, lighted areas, a kitchen, and even a nap room. It was a home away from home. It was pleasant because there was no competition, the idea was to help and share, not to be better than the next student. This gave you an opportunity to bond with your classmates.

We had a real variety of students. One from Singapore, three from Alaska, a Military wife, a man married to a Japanese

THE FINAL COMMANDMENTS

Professor, a Jewish lady who's husband was Government, a Hawaiian that went on to get her law degree, and my good buddy Sandy Jones. Sandy already worked in a Hospital Library and was finishing her degree. We met in an odd way. In Business School I studied Quality Circles and still belonged to an organization. She was doing research and asked about getting information. Someone told her to talk with me, I was involved with them. She never had the opportunity to set and talk with us between classes, as she went back to work. "How, will I know her?" she asked. They told her to just listen for the loudest with a big laugh. That was our first introduction.

There was no fooling around at the Rhino Bar now. All my roommates had left, and it was strictly study and get my degree. I had letters waiting from Seif, thus starting a 17,000 mile relationship. There is something special about being in love by mail. You rush to your mailbox, being ecstatic when you receive a letter, and depressed when one doesn't come. I took extra classes to complete my degree early.

I had made arrangements to do research in Egypt during the Christmas break on Preservation and Conversation of Library Materials. This would also give me extra credits. With a paper due every week, extra credits, working part time at the Environmental Library, and corresponding with Seif, the months just disappeared.

It was time to make reservations for my trip to Egypt. There would be no joy in the trip. You took off from Honolulu on a Friday, and landed in Cairo on Monday. I only good thing about the trip was I could put my bags on and hope to see them in Cairo, without having to drag them around at every airport. TWA was the best schedule, plus now I had a free trip from my mileage points from around the world. Then they had direct flights from New York, so you only had to make three stops getting there. You always hoped you didn't get on the plane with the Indian woman dragging five children under six years old on the plane. There was no place you could sit that you couldn't hear one of the children crying. There would be five meals and three movies. It was like a moving city. You'd get to know the life stories of everyone within 10 seats of you, and offer your wine to the one that looks like they needed it the most.

Although I had only been to Egypt once for a few months, I acted like an ex-pat, someone that has lived abroad and knows the country very well, by informing the first timers where to shop, and some important customs. Maybe I could move there, it felt just like I was going home. The excitement I felt when I saw the pyramid magnificence in the sky brought back all the thoughts of shopping, eating, and mingling with the people. It's actually the first time I'd had to stop and think since the semester was over.

There were the regular lines, delays, questions, and finally getting your bags. No one could come into the terminal, so I had no way of knowing if Seif was there or not. The plane of course was hours late. "No, I don't want a taxi, I just want my bags to go outside" I kept repeating as everyone wanted you to use their service. I finally got outside about 2 A.M. I stood as close to the curb as possible hoping to be recognized. It was about an hour before Seif arrived. The meeting was not what I had hoped after all our passionate letters. His car had broken down and of course there was no way to notify me.

The ride back was not pleasant. How come I brought so many suitcases? I told him I had to do some research and had books and papers. The rest of the conversation was about the car, about the problems he was having with his brother-in-law, and his mother and aunt. I was so tired I really didn't care, I just wanted to sleep.

The bawwab dragged the suitcases up. I wondered why they were always so small and old. I always felt guilty having them try to drag my heavy suitcases.

We went straight to bed, sleeping in the same bed that was a gift to his family from King Farouk. I assumed us sleeping together meant is mother wasn't back yet. I woke up hearing a beautiful French voice rattling some dishes. This lovely lady had brought in breakfast and tea. I didn't understand a word she said, but just kept nodding and saying iywa, iywa. I thought it was the maid and wondered what she thought about me being in Seif's bed with no top on.

Seif had already been up for morning prayers. They do a special preparation of washing the body for prayers. He had just returned when the breakfast had come. He turned to me and said, "mother says you have beautiful eyes." I couldn't think. That was his mother serving us? My first meeting of his mother was going to be in King Farouk's bed, in a county where men and women aren't even allowed to hold hands? How could I ever face her?

I was so uncomfortable in the situation, not being able to communicate with anyone but Seif. I felt shame each time I was with his mother and aunt. But they seemed fine, and very friendly.

I would find out later that they thought we were married. In fact, I could have been married and not even know it. I didn't know if there was a civil ceremony for this, but as a foreigner, you don't have to be present to be married. Later on in my research I would discover there were special circumstances for some sort of quick marriages.

There was a time before President Sadat's wife helped change some of the laws, women didn't even have to be aware they were divorced. He just had to say I divorce you three times and it was over. Now you have to get together with both families and try to save the marriage. There is no negotiation regarding money or the children. That is all set before you marry. That's why the women's parents won't let her get married until all the furniture is purchased and in place. Also they will haggle for months over how much jewelry he must give her. This is because this is the only thing she will have after the marriage. Even the children are given to the father at a certain age, since he is responsible for the religion.

The flat had furniture stacked all over. Seif's aunt was married to a doctor who had passed away. A woman cannot live by herself, even if she is an adult, so Seif moved his younger brother in to live with her. When President Nasser came into power he made rules about people having more than one flat and not living in them. They didn't have enough housing, and your flat could be given to someone else to ease the housing problem. The brother moved out, since he had his own family. Seif tried to get his sisters husband to stay over there, and he refused to leave his family. They lost the flat, and that's what all the furniture was about. Our soap operas have nothing on their family matters!

I was happy to get out and start my research. The American University is closed on Friday, the Moslem holy day, and Sunday, the Christian Holiday. The American Embassy was closed on Friday and Saturday, and opened Sunday through Thursday. The phones didn't work, there were no phone books, so the only way to make contact was through another person. After Seif left for work, I left a note telling him I was going to AUC to start my research. When I arrived, the bawwab told me it was closed. I didn't know what to do. As I turned away, he asked, "American?" I turned and said aywa. He gestured for me to follow him. We went to the cub and he stopped a cab. I heard him say American Embassy, and couldn't think of any other alternative.

It was only a few blocks away, and we arrived at several buildings with walls around them. I went to the gate and the Marine said, "Who do you wish to see please?" I told him I doubt if anyone I wanted to see would be there today with it being Sunday. He said the Embassy is open on Sunday. I explained I needed information about libraries in Egypt. "You would probably want to speak with the Library of Congress" he replied. My heart skipped a beat. "We have a branch over here?" " It's not really a branch, it's what they call Overseas Operation, for ordering books. Would you like to be put in contact with them? They're not actually in the compound, but a few blocks away. I'll call them if you like." I told them I hadn't found a phone yet that worked. He laughed and said they had their own internal phone service. He had called the Field Director, and he told me to come to the office.

The one thing about Egypt, it appears people always have time for tea. You must come and have tea. They were housed in a beautiful Villa about two blocks from the embassy. I can see why the area is called Garden City.

The Field Director was an academic, and you could tell by his manner he had been there a long time. He had picked up their habits of yelling harshly at the workers in Arabic. He was very gracious and helpful. Through workers going by taxi to send messages, he had set me up with several organizations to do my research. Also next week a gentlemen from the Library of Congress in D.C. was coming to AUC to speak on copyright laws. He would get me an invitation.

It felt so good to be around people I could actually communicate with, and start my research. I was so excited, I could hardly wait to tell Seif of my accomplishments.

Before I could even tell him about my research he yelled, "where have you been, and don't tell me the University! It's closed today."

I hadn't even replied, he ordered me to set down with his mother and aunt, and not to leave. He had to do something. I could tell by looking at his mother, he'd been yelling at her.

After he stormed out, they sat me down and fed me. I smiled at them, and they smiled at me. His mother took me by the hand over to the tape machine. She started playing music from Hawaii, and pointed to me, Hawaii? Iywa, iywa, I said, and said shukran, thank you. I started moving with the music, and they laughed and clapped. I went into a swaying hula and they clapped some more. They got up with me and tried to follow me. I spent the evening teaching them the hula. We all laughed and had a wonderful evening.

I heard a soft knock at the door, it was the bawwab. Apparently she'd asked him to let her know when Seif came back. She swiftly turned off the tape machine and led us to the sofa. She was scared of him! She was scared of her own son! I looked at the three of us setting there waiting for the master to return. It was in a harem!

Just when you think it can't get worse, it unquestionably does. I heard a child crying, being yelled at. The door opens and Seif is dragging in a child with his sister following him crying. He doesn't even introduce us, but takes them back to one of the rooms. The flats are actually larger than a home. They are half of one whole floor. She was being taken to the very back, which I hadn't even seen yet. Add one more to the harem!

The best I could understand he was mad at his brother-in-law for not moving over with his aunt. He is bringing his sister and her son back to live with him until this matter is settled. Don't ask, they do have that power. She has to do what he says since the father is dead.

This was not the romantic setting I was expecting. When I left, he was kissing the tears from my eyes, now he is yelling at me like I have no rights. A terrible thought came to me. What if I really was married to him, I couldn't even leave the country!

He was so busy yelling at everyone we didn't even make love. He only took breaks to do his prayers. In all fairness to him, this was a big responsibility, being responsible for everyone. He had to return from England and not finish his education when his father died. Their family had gone from being Pasha's in the King's circle of friends to having the government take their property. It couldn't be a very pleasant situation. He had turned to his religion and when ever you questioned him about something, he would reply, "the Koran says....." and he knows I couldn't read Arabic and know what it says.

He ordered me not to leave when he went to work. I told him I had to do my research. "Forget your research, forget your degree. Mohammed has instructions not to let you out" and he slammed the door. I was scared now, I thought of Marianne almost getting beat up.

I heard his mother make a phone call. She led me to the bedroom and helped me start packing and made the sign to be quiet. Then I heard her yell for Mohammed and give him a big list of things to get. A few minutes later Ahmed was at the door. We cut our five-minute greeting short. He took my bags himself to the car since Mohammed was gone.

When we were in the car I didn't know what to say. He apologized to me, he had no idea Seif would be mean. Apparently Seif's aunt was related to Ahmed through the marriage. So he was not a blood relative. His aunt was aware Ahmed knew his mother and she had called for help. He asked me whom my research would be with. I had mentioned the people, and we went to what they call a central telephone service. You give them money and go in a phone booth. They'll just cut you off at the end of the money, instead of collecting more later. He called one of the organizations and arranged for me to do part of the research at Luxor in Upper Egypt. I needed to get out of town until Seif settles down. There's something about pride, and he has to defend his pride.

We had lunch with Helen, and later they took me to the airport to go to Luxor. Helen gave me a small bag to take, and took my things and kept them until I came back. Ahmed wrote me a note in Arabic with directions to an inexpensive Hotel in Zamalek when I came back.

Someone met me at the airport and spoke excellent English. I was so happy, and it was an extra treat to be able to see the tombs in the Valley of the Kings and Queens. I stayed on a

THE FINAL COMMANDMENTS

houseboat on the Nile, it belonged to the company I would be doing research with.

Since I needed to stay away from Cairo as long as I could, I had the opportunity to help with a dig. The University of Pennsylvania has a large Egyptology program and was working on this location for years. When you remove things from a dig, they must be cataloged and identified. They couldn't continue until certain things had been cataloged. What an opportunity! I would be cataloging everything from broken pottery to ten-ton stones.

My host for my research, Hassen Fahmy, had asked if I was going to upper Egypt and visit Aswan Dam and Abu Simbel? I hadn't originally planned it as I was going to save my free time to spend with Seif. Since this would be my last trip to Egypt, I'd better see as much as I could. I told Hassen I hadn't made any plans.

I have to go up to Aswan to check on our shop. You're welcome to come with me and I can be your private guide. He smiled at this. Then to make sure he wasn't misunderstood, he added his cousin runs one of the hotels and he can get me a good rate on a room.

Hassen had been a great relief from my situation with Seif. Although he was just a business associate, if Seif saw me with him, he'd have a confrontation for his pride. This reminded be of a newspaper clipping I had just read in the Egyptian Gazette. A married woman was setting in a car talking with a male co-worker, in broad daylight with 13 million people walking by. She was very distressed about a fight she'd had with her husband and a co-worker was trying to comfort her. She didn't want to cry in the office, so he had gone to the car with her.

He husband saw her, pulled out a tiny pocketknife and stabbed the man to death. In the courts he got off as it wasn't a "real" weapon and his wife was in public with the man. When I tried to discuss this with Seif he said of course the courts were right. That was his wife, and she was in public with another man, no matter what the circumstances were.

Hassen was so interesting to talk with. His family was very influential. His Uncle was an Ambassador, and his father held some government post. He was trained at the Military Academy. What happened when President Nasser took over, the power shifted from the Pasha's and educated business class. Land was re-distributed, and the power went from the upper elite to the Military. There of course were problems with the distribution of wealth, as with every county. President Nasser meant well, and wanted Egypt to be for the Egyptians. He tried to divide up the land, giving the workers land. This didn't work for two reasons. First, the aristocrats just put the land under other relative's names. By dividing the land into smaller parcel's, you couldn't produce as much. The workers only knew how to farm the land, nothing about managing money, or marketing. Egypt, which use to be the breadbasket for the Middle East, is now importing their food. In truth, the wealth was just switched from the aristocrats to the military.

Hassen, being of the new Military class, was afforded privileges of the ruling class. He was trained in the Military as Special Forces, which gave him the opportunity to be one of the first Egyptians to go to Israel with President Sadat for the Peace Conference. This was a big honor, as the Arab Nations had set a rule that no Moslem could go to Israel until it was defeated. When President Sadat made the Peace Agreement, the Arab countries said they would not fly any plane marked Egypt Air since it had landed on Israel soil. This is the saving face of the Arab world. Egypt just took so many planes and renamed them Air Sinai, and the Arabs would use those to come for vacation in Egypt.

Hassen had traveled extensively, and knew how to get things done. He was defiantly a take charge person. He had our tickets, reservations, and everything ready the next day. I was beginning to relax and enjoy myself. It's the first time I had looked at Hassen as a man instead of business associate. He was handsome in a different way from Seif. Hassen was light skinned, straight hair, and almost blue eyes. Seif was of Turkish background, therefore the Mediterranean features. In the history of Egypt there's been several conquers. A local military cast called the Mamluks took control in 1250 and still governed after the conquest by Ottoman Turks in 1517. When the British seized control of Egypt's government in 1882, they let the Ottoman Empire still govern until 1914.

Hassen let it be clear that he was a Pharonic Egyptian, meaning of the pure blood from the Pharos. Egypt's largest populations were a mixture of Greek, Turkish, French, Armenian, and British. The aristocrats spoke French and Arabic. Later on when we took over from Russia for Egyptian foreign aid, English became a necessity.

Hassen really related to the local people. President Sadat was from upper Egypt, that is why he was so dark. It's on the border of Sudan, and many have migrated from Africa. They are referred to as Nubian, and probably would be considered the people of the soil, farmers. They treated Hassen as if he was President Sadat himself. I laughed for hours at their stories. It is common, almost a rule, that they intermarry with cousins. The privileged do it to control the money, keep it in the family. I told them they're places in the United States where it was against the law to marry your cousin. They all gasped in disbelief, and one gapped his heart like he was having a heart attack. With their grand gestures of expression, he said, "Not marry my cousin? I would rather die than that be able to marry Mona!" Then they asked me why such a silly law? I didn't want to explain about what it does to the bloodline, and just said " ma'lash", which is what you always answer when you don't know what else to say. It really means it doesn't matter. They were so pleased that I knew a couple of Arab words, and kept complementing on how wonderful my Arabic was.

We had to spend half a day there, as we had to have tea. You have ten people running all over to get sweets and fruit to set up the table. It is like high tea with the Queen.

We finally had to beg our leave or we wouldn't have time to see the dam and the lake. It was as if we had known each other all our lives. "When will you be back to see us? We miss you so much. My heart will ache until I see your blue eyes again," they each cried with almost tears in their eyes.

The hotel was on a beautiful lake. We hadn't even checked in yet. My room had a beautiful view of the lake, and it was so peaceful. I was seeing the beauty in Egypt again. Hassen had suggested since we were limited for time that we combine a picnic with a boat ride to see the island in the middle of the lake. I don't know what would have happened if I'd say no, as the boat, picnic basket, and everything was ready to go. It was rather nice to have someone take charge and not have to worry about anything.

THE FINAL COMMANDMENTS

It was so beautiful and peaceful. Other than their regular beautiful sing-song greeting, the boatman never said another word. He was in front of us, and didn't understand English. "I enjoy these quiet moments very much, there is so much noise and tourist, it is wonderful to be in the Egypt of thousands of years ago" Hassen commented. I agreed, and just leaned back to relax. The seat wasn't high enough to hold my head, and Hassen put his arm there to make it comfortable. It just seemed natural. I had my hand in the warm water, and was looking up at the birds above. This must be what Cleopatra felt like when she was on her barge.

We got to the island, and were dropped off. The boat took off, but I didn't question it. It was too pleasant a place to worry about anything. There was a tent set up for shade and pillows around to eat Bedouin style. It was indeed a feast. I had jokingly said to Hassen how wonderful it would be just to live here, just laugh and eat all the time. He brought me back to reality. You could no longer live your life just for comfort than I could. There are some of us that are chosen to do certain things in our lives. President Sadat was one of the chosen. He gave his life. All we can do is find certain moments in our lives that have special meaning, and hang on to them in our memories. So much for day dreaming. He really was a serious person. We managed to lay in the sun and take a little nap. He reminded me, that although we were on what seemed to be an isolated island, there were always people watching you. I would remember this apprehensive feeling of being watched after they passed the Patriot Act in the United States. In truth, our government would be able to come in our home without us even knowing and we'd never know.

The sun was going down when the boatman came back. It was a quiet time returning. We'd made arrangement to have a late dinner, giving me a change to take a little nap. When I met Hassen in the lobby, I almost didn't recognize him. He was dressed in a suit, and looked like something out of a man's magazine. I hadn't noticed how handsome he was! We had a wonderful meal, sat outside for an after dinner non-alcoholic drink, and listened to the sounds of the evening.

"So what do you think of upper Egypt and me?" The question took me by surprise. I laughed and replied, "Do you think the answer will be the same for both?" He simply said yes. "Then I would have to say it has been a wonderful time in my life, a calm and emotion I haven't experienced before. As you mentioned, a special moment in my life to hang on to in my memories." He took my hand under the table and held it, as he leaned over and put his lips next to my ear. He whispered, "Who knows, there might be more moments through our lifetime." He was gently rubbing my hand.

It's getting late, and you have to go to Abu Simbel tomorrow. I won't be going with you. However, I want you to know I will be watching after you while you're in Egypt, no matter where you are. He left me at the front desk. I really didn't want to part, but he had told me in so many words about the customs and being up too late together. I wanted to kiss him goodnight, but I knew I couldn't. He gave me a handshake. If this was any other county I could send signals. Then I heard the phrase, " ma'asalama."

I felt so empty. I wanted more memories. I looked out on my balcony and saw a full moon. How romantic. A falling star, make a wish. I wish Hassan was making love to me as I looked out at the moon, a real memory to take with me. What planet are you living on? He has already taken two days and showed you wonderful Upper Egypt. You don't even know how he feels about you. They are so polite you can't tell if they really like you or not.

I took a long, hot bath. As I came out I heard music. That was funny, I'd looked all over and couldn't find a radio. I looked at the balcony and saw Hassan's outline from the moon. He turned and had his finger up to his lips, signaling me not to speak. I was wondering how he got in, then I remembered he was Special Forces.

I moved next to him at the balcony and he positioned himself behind me. As he pressed his body against me, there was no doubt why he was here. My heart was beating so fast I couldn't even think. His hands gently reached around and started massaging my breasts. Then his tongue was in my ear. This is out of sequence, we hadn't even kissed yet. He picked me up and carried me to the bed. I heard the singer say something about this moment will last forever. For sure his travels covered more than Government business. He found spots I didn't even know I had.

I've heard of marathon love making, but this is the first time it's happened to me. I think it only stopped because the sun was coming up. He got up to go to the bathroom and I think I feel asleep. I woke when the sun hit my eyes. There was no sign of him even being there. Maybe it was a dream!

The phone rang, it was Hassan. "Good morning, I trust you had a good sleep? I'll meet you in the courtyard for breakfast in thirty minutes" click. No five minutes of greetings, no answer to his question, nothing! The most memorial night of my life and I can't even acknowledge it. Or maybe there was nothing last night? I've heard about some of their teas that make you hallucinate. Maybe I drank some of that tea?

We had breakfast with his cousin, the Manager of the hotel. Very polite, about how I had drank from the Nile and I would return. He had to excuse himself, but please stay and enjoy the rest of our breakfast in his private gazebo. To find any privacy in Egypt was remarkable.

I felt Hassan hand going around my waist. "I trust you had a pleasant sleep" he said with a sheepish grin. It wasn't a dream, it was real! Rather I saw him again or not, I would always have that one night. "I don't have much time, your plane leaves shortly. I'm having Mahmoud drive you to the airport. I'm afraid I'd grab you and kiss you in front of everyone. As you know, that couldn't be allowed in Egypt. I have so much to say, and so little time. I can say this, I can be where I want to be. I don't have to be in Upper Egypt. I have chosen it. Now you have come and messed up my thoughts. I'll see you in Cairo before you leave. Here is a phone number if you're ever in any trouble. The code will be something about meeting Mahmoud in Upper Egypt. You will be in my life. Our destiny is intertwined. He took my hand and turned it over, and started kissing it.

I went to pack, and didn't see him again. Mahmoud drove me to the airport, and to my surprise, came with me to be my guide at Abu Simbel.

I thought nothing could amaze me after seeing the Pyramids, but these figures carved into a mountain, 65 feet tall, being there for over 3,500 year was impressive. They are of Ramesses as a young boy, youth, young man, and mature statesman. What an enormous ego Ramesses the Great must have had. The location is in the wasteland almost on the Nubian boarder. He would have had to bring many thousand of workers up there in the hot heat for many years to make this monument to himself.

I returned to Cairo just in time for the conference at AUC on copyright laws. How stimulating it was. I met the professionals in universities and libraries. One of the Professors from Cairo University, the Egyptian University, set up an appointment for me to visit his University. He told me how much they needed people like myself to bring Egypt up to date. Later I would make arrangements with him to come back and do my Ph.D., with him as my advisor. He could get me a position with the government while working on my Ph.D. Egypt was so exciting, they were just starting their information revolution. What a wonderful opportunity to be at the start of setting up the system for the government.

There was a Professor doing research at the Nag Hammadi Library, which I had to admit I'd never heard of before. This was a collection of over fifty texts, which was discovered in Upper Egypt in 1945. These would later be proof that the bible had been edited and altered

If I were here I wouldn't only be dealing with the future, but also the past. How could any place be more exciting for a librarian? I actually now had a reason for my degree, not just earning money, but doing something important!

What a stimulating evening. There were about twenty people in Egypt working on their Doctoral Degree preparing papers. Every night you could go and listen to one of them speak. What an exciting place Egypt was! The beginning of civilization, and now getting ready to catch up with technology. It was a love affair now. I forgot the phones didn't work, nothing was done on schedule, or the fact you never really knew if someone liked you or was being polite. Their culture was so polite, they had you thinking you were the most important person in their life.

Just when I thought life couldn't get any better, there was Hassan waiting inside my room when I got home. I defiantly know he used some back way to get there. I remember the instance of the couple I'd met through friends at the hostel. She'd fallen in love with a Palestinian in the United States and they were going back to the West Bank to teach. Somewhere along the way he was offered a job in Saudi Arabia for a big salary and accepted. She of course couldn't go. They were going to spend as much time as possible in Egypt before they went their separate ways. They had gotten separate rooms in the same hotel. Although he was not Egyptian, and she was an American, they made sure they didn't spend any time together. The office would call each room about every two hours to see if they needed anything, what time they wanted breakfast, etc. I don't know what would have happened if they hadn't answered their phone in there own rooms. I'm sure the Morals Police was on alert. Alert all Morals Police, there's another American woman trying to corrupt a Moslem man.

Hassan was a pure physical attraction, I'll admit it. We didn't even say hello. It probably took thirty seconds to get our clothes off. It's like you know your going to die in six hours, and you want every second to count. After two hours when we took a breather, he turned and looked at me and said, "Natasha, what have you done to me? I can't think, I can't sleep, I can do nothing but think of touching you. You are in my heart, my eyes, under my skin. I'm tied to you through my sole. I cannot bear to think of your body being so far from me. What's the latest you can leave?" I told Hassan I had to leave on my scheduled flight to make it back for my classes. "It looks like I'll have to follow you to the end of the earth to make love again." When I woke up, he was gone again. I didn't see or hear from him again before I left.

Never had anyone needed a vacation from a vacation as much as I did. My body and mind was completely drained. But my enthusiasm was batting 100. I was looking forward to getting my degree finished, going back to Egypt for my Ph.D., and becoming involved in an exciting project. I wouldn't have time to worry about a personal life. Besides, I had memories stored up for a lifetime.

7

———

RETURN TO THE LAND
OF THE PHAROS

I t's a real cultural shock coming from the barren desert of Egypt to Hawaii where beautiful green vegetation surrounds you, and cool breezes are always keeping you comfortable. Even though Hawaiians think there island is overcrowded, it's nothing like Egypt where walking in the streets is even a problem. You never hear horns honking, and drivers stop and waive you on. However, my thoughts won't be on the beautiful weather, as I'll be doubling up on classes to finish earlier.

One of my big research projects was to make a bibliography. Since I was active with the United Nations at the time, I decided to do it on peace organizations. I couldn't believe the

THE FINAL COMMANDMENTS

results! Thousand and thousands of organizations, one of the sadists being children's concerns over death and war. This was in 1983. I remember seeing a published research by Transcendental Meditation participants proving a population as small as 1% in an area meditating could reduce violent crimes. A study of a random sample of 160 U.S. cities showed over a 7-year period back in the late 70s reductions in the crime rate as high as 23%.

I've come across this information again and again in my recent research. There are millions of people looking for any way to stop these world conflicts and the billions of useless dollars being spent, plus the human toll on lives.

From 1981 to 1983 the Maharishi International University had a branch in D.C., and using the transfer function approach of time series analysis at the College of Natural Law and decreased violent crimes in Washington over the two-year study. When the College of Natural Law moved from Washington in 1986-87, the homicides in Washington, D.C. increased to become the highest in the nation in 1990. A group of 4,000 participants in the TM programs assembled there from June 7 to July 30, 1993 to demonstrate that levels of violent crime would fall during the project. There was a 27 member Project Review Board of independent scientists, leading citizens, and weekly input from the District of Columbia Metropolitan Police Department on crime data from FBI Crime Reports. The analysis showed that homicides, rapes and assaults crimes dropped 23.3%. In that area, even Senators are getting mugged on the streets.

Sounds so easy, just meditate the world's troubles away. I remember last semester when I was looking for an easy course and took one on quieting your mind. The syllabus looked like a slam-dunk. You are to meditate and empty your mind of any thoughts. It turned out to be the hardest course I've ever taken. Have you ever tried not to have one thought? I'll work on saving the world later, for now, just let me get through my Graduate work.

Time was swiftly passing. Charles, my Marketing Professor, was going to help plan the graduation party. One of the students worked at the Aquarium in Waikiki and would be able to have it there in the evening. I actually ended up with four of my old boyfriends there, and didn't quite know how I was going to work it. Hassen and I had been corresponding and I'd just mentioned in passing about the graduation date and did he want to attend? I of course was joking, who would fly 17,000 miles to come to a graduation party? To my surprise, he said yes! When I nonchalantly mentioned it to Charles he said, "Well that's nice, looks like you'll have more than one date for the graduation." Little did he know there were two others besides Hassen.

I believe this was my first critical path for scheduling. I had finals to study for, a guest coming that I had to arrange entertainment and housing, graduation party to plan, packing up and moving half way around the world, and arranging all financial matters before leaving.

Katie came over only for the party. After my last commencement she stated no one should have to set through another one. The guest speaker was some Washington bureaucrat, drunk, and rattled on and on for what seemed hours in the hot sun.

My bridge partner from Pakistan took Hassen on the island tour while I did my finals. Finally it was over. Surely the University was suppose to be more fun than this.

THE FINAL COMMANDMENTS

I never really took a breather till we stopped in California to see my son Jordan, and my two grandsons. Hassen stayed long enough to see Disney Land and shop. He took back two over sized boxes full of reference books for me.

It wasn't until I was on the plane headed for Egypt that I realized what I was doing. At that very moment, the plane was my home! It just dawned on me, I didn't have one key. I didn't own anything! Talk about going the way of the Buddha and simplicity. The Law of Conscious Detachment, Buddha stating resistance causes suffering. How many people would ever be able to say that? They owned not one key. I wasn't going for a vacation, I was moving with all my possessions in two bags 17,000 miles to the other side of the world. I had no home to go to, or a home to go back to. This must be the part where the General informs his men to burn the bridges, as there is no retreat. I'm forty-five years old, no home, no job, no keys, setting on a plane over the Atlantic, just having my tea and crumpets. I just kept reminding my self to think positive!

I knew Hassen was back in Luxor, so they'd me no one to meet me. As usual, it was about 2 A.M. by the time I cleared customs. I was too tired to negotiate the taxi fare and just accepted whatever they said. I stayed at the Pension again, at least that would be familiar territory. Mohammed remembered me and spent five minutes greeting me. There was a new clerk. No he had not received my reservation, and would have to see what he could do. The room of course would be more expensive as the rate I had before were all taken. I looked at Mohammed and he shook his head no. I excused myself to go to the restroom, and checked my old room on the way back. It was vacant. "I notice my old room is still open" I informed him. By the way, have a message sent to Pasha Aziz, he will be happy to see me again. His eyebrows went up at the mention of his name, and gave me the room at the regular rate.

I just slept for two days, really trying to figure out what I should do next. I tried to contact my advisor at Cairo University, but of course the phones weren't working. I took a taxi to the University the next day and couldn't get on campus. The security is you need to be a student or have a signed letter to see someone. I explained I couldn't get through by phone. He shrugged his shoulders and said, 'ma'alesh.' This was going nowhere fast.

I waited outside and stopped someone that spoke English and asked him if he knew Professor. Yes, yes, of course, we take tea together. Would he take this message to him and have him call me, it's very important. By of course, no, no, you need not give me any money…well, if you insist. Shukran.

I waited three days and no message. Pasha Aziz was so happy to see me back. Let's have tea and finish our wonderful conversations. I knew I had to leave this place. But where could I go. At customs coming in I told them I could be reached through Cairo University and gave this address. I could end up in jail if the University doesn't enroll me and I'm not staying here! Even worse, I really didn't know enough of the language to even communicate with anyone.

I was in Zamalek having lunch and thought maybe Helen is still at the Hostel! No, she finished last semester, unless she decided to do some Graduate work. So I walked down to the Hostel on the Nile. The minute the bawwab saw me he started the five minute greeting. It was as if I was his long lost relative he had been searching for all his life. He spoke some English, and I asked about Helen. Iywa, iywa! Then he took my hand and started down to the main street. No, you don't understand, I'm looking for Helen, my girlfriend. Iywa, iywa, as he pulled me down the street I know he had good intentions, and I didn't want to hurt his feelings, so I just followed him. He led me around the corner, and started a greeting with another bawwab. The other bawwab started leading me up some stairs. How do I get out of this one? He knocked on a door, and when it opened, there stood Helen.

I don't think I have ever been so happy to see someone. I know she's not an emotional person, but I grabbed her and hugged her anyway. We both said to each other in unison, "what are you doing here?" and started laughing.

Helen and Ahmed were going to get married. They would have to wait till his sister Mona was married. Her finance was in Kuwait saving money. They can't get married until all the furniture and appliances are purchased and in the flat. Then Ahmed will have the flat to himself and can get married.

I told her about coming back to get my Ph.D. at Cairo University and not being able to find my advisor. I told her I had to get away from the Pasha again. "You could probably rent a studio here for a month or so. They're small, but in a good location. There's an Italian Doctor that owns them, and she's like the dragon lady. But, once she gets her money, she leaves you alone. Mustafa is the bawwab and he's really good, he'll watch out for you."

I rented the flat, and went to the Mugamba Building to give my new address. My love affair with Egypt was fading. It took so long to get anything done. It took me half a day standing in line to take care of this small matter.

LUTISHA TESAREK

We were lucky to have a phone extension in our rooms. Some people have been waiting over six years for a phone. It wasn't private, there were about three of us on the line, but at least we had a line, when it worked.

Maybe the Field Director from the Library of Congress could help me locate Professor Salah. I went to the office and was so happy to be around people that I could communicate with. Of course we had tea, and about two hours went by before I asked for his help. He tried the phone with no luck. He sent a worker in a taxi with a note. We discussed the projects at LOC, and he mentioned he would be transferring back to Washington, D.C. in a few months. He had many reports that needed to be done, the American way, and their Accountant didn't seem to understand what he was talking about.

The worker came back. Just when you think it can't get worse, it does! The return note stated Professor Ahmed Salah was of the good fortune to become a visiting Professor in Saudi Arabia. This was good news for him, as he would be making about 100 times what he makes in Egypt. That's why everyone goes to the oil Middle East countries to work and send money home for the families.

The Field Director could see my distress. Why hadn't he written me and informed me? I could see he knew exactly what I was thinking. You must understand Natasha, in this culture they are so polite, they say what they think you want to hear. He probably forgot in the excitement of the new position to inform you and arrange another advisor he said as he looked down at his tea cup.

He yelled harshly at the tea man and asked him to move our tea into his office. He probably thought I was going to start crying or something. We continued our conversation in his office with the door closed. "Look, I'm sure this will be straightened out before the next semester starts. You've already taken a flat in Zamalek? I live in Zamalek also. You'd mentioned you have an accounting degree. Would you like to work a few months here and help me with these reports? We have a new Field Director coming in six months, and I have to tell him exactly what needs to be done to bring this office up to date. I know nothing about computers. You'd be doing me a favor." I was still numb, and couldn't really think at this moment. Susan had been trying to get a job at the Embassy for over a year, she said it was next to impossible. Now I was being offered a position. I know have an apartment, and a position. That's two keys! Things were looking brighter.

Thus started my life as an ex-pat in Egypt. These are people caught between two cultures, they can't live comfortably in either. The State Department realizes this and has a debriefing for their employees when they rotate back to the States. The length of time to a post is just long enough that the employees don't get attached to the country or it's people.

The position was so interesting that nothing else mattered. For the first time I felt really in charge of my work. Computers not hooked up to mainframes, or stand alone as they were called in the beginning, were so new no one knew anything about them. I was top dog.

Then I found out about T.G.I.T. hosted by the Marines. Since the Embassy is closed Friday and Saturday, they celebrate Thursday nights. The Marines had their barracks right on the compound, and opened their common area for a party once a week. Talk about a mixture of misfits! Besides the Embassy employees, there were oilmen, several different American companies working on military projects, and foreign officials. A big pool table was in the center of the room, and a jukebox for dancing. Of course you had your spooks pretending to be working on some AID project to see what they could pick up. I would guess Cairo was the spy capitol of the Middle East.

It was stimulating to be around so much energy. I wasn't aware of the unwritten rule that you don't ask someone what project they are working on. About half the people there were working on top secret military projects. If they were walking around with a briefcase handcuffed to them, you definitely stayed away from the conversation.

I heard a clipped British accent from behind me say, "Would you like to dance mate?" I turned to see a very well dressed gentleman with a dazzling smile. He could have come straight from Wall Street. I had heard his voice all evening, laughing loudly and telling jokes. He certainly wasn't the typical restrained Englishman. "Vern Evans, the Queen's messenger at your service" he said laughingly and dragged me to the dance floor. You certainly didn't have to worry about something to say, as he talked constantly. It wasn't would you like to, but we are going to go to the Hilton after this and finish the night off.

It was actually nice to be around someone not so serious, not talking about his projects and problems with communication. I went with the crowd of ex-pats and finished off the night with them. They were loud and drunk, but since they tipped big the hotel was glad to see then. They were treated like royalty, so they must go there quit often. We went for breakfast afterward at the El Salam Hyatt Hotel, which took us to sunrise. I started to get up and say goodbye, and Vern did his loud laugh again.

THE FINAL COMMANDMENTS

"What are you talking about, the week-end has just begun. We're going swimming now. Abdullah, go get the manager to open the dress shop, we have a customer." I thought this guy is really over the edge. As I turn around I see the manager running with a handful of keys in his hands. "Mr. Vern, how are you? Please, follow me." I knew enough about the culture to know it would be an insult to the Manager for his hospitality if I didn't go. Vern picked out a bathing suit, a couple of galabeyya's, and an evening dress. "I can't accept these!" I said. "Of course not, just leave them in the room for the next time you come." "I'm not going to a hotel room with you," I replied. "Oh, you don't understand. This is my home and office, I rent a suite here. My company feels for security and other reasons, it's better than setting up a flat. Mahmud, just send those to my suite." He takes my arm and says, " we're only going to swim, then there's a party tonight. I thought it would be easier for you just to stay here instead of dealing with the traffic. Anytime you want to go home, I'll have my driver take you. You're in the driver's seat, whatever you want, whenever you want it. The Queens Messenger at your service." He laughs and salutes at me. Apparently he didn't take anything seriously.

Everyone was at the pool, 7 A.M. drinking the local Stella Beer, which I head was compared to horse pee. About 9 A.M. they all passed out and slept in the deck chairs till late afternoon. Apparently this was a regular routine, as all the servants kept making sure there cigarettes were put out, and kept switching the umbrellas for shade as the sun patterns changed. There was an Egyptian show that night, and again the round of drinking, dancing, and telling jokes. This was a fun crowd, they were loud, but no one started fighting. They would just pass out and be carried to their rooms. I didn't drink, and I knew how bad I felt just from lack of sleep. I can't imagine how they felt when they got up the next morning. They laughed at me when they found out I didn't drink and said they felt sorry for me. I looked at them questionable. When you wake up, that's the best your going to feel. We know it has to get better, and they all laughed.

I told Vern I needed to get back, I couldn't take another day of fun, I had to rest up for work. He had is driver take me back to Zamalek. My first time out at a social event turned out to be almost two days.

I got a call from one of the Marines I'd met telling me Wild Bruce was having a party next weekend. He was an oilman that wore a leather jacket with the fringe and cowboy boots and of course cowboy hat. Being from Tulsa he got thrown out for having a fight with someone from Texas. He was always smiling, laughing, and had a drink in his hand. But of course, this fit the description of 80% of the party people. His flat was right behind the Marriott Hotel, so it was only a few blocks from my place. At least I wouldn't have to stay for the weekend, I could walk home.

This was a different type of crowd, computer geeks and second level managers. Then there was the locals that love to come for the free drinks. He had some military personnel who's project was in a town called Fayoum, about 60 miles away, and they also stayed in a hotel called the Jolly Ville out by the pyramids. I've always loved parties and dancing, so this made Egypt more interesting. I'd go to the Jolly Ville Hotel when there wasn't any parties and take my slow cooker and fix dinner. I really missed having a place to cook and entertain, thus I became the roving gourmet. I'd cook for all the parties. The electricity in Egypt has a different current, and we had to use transformers with our electrical devices. But I guess we overloaded it, as I blew the electricity at the hotel and wasn't invited back to cook. Later on when there was a coup the Jolly Ville was one of the hotels burned down by the Pyramids. Then the Air Force was sent to Fayoum and they weren't too pleased.

A third circle of friends was the bridge club. These were all Egyptians, mostly diplomats. We played at their Country Club. I started dating a diplomat that had just returned from Washington, D.C. His name was Atia Atia. Yes, that is correct. If your wondering why so many of the Moslem first and last names are the same, it's because when their named, there first name is the given name, the second their fathers, the third their grandfathers, and the fourth their village or type of work. I loved the movie 'Isthar' with Warren Beatty when he was telling someone to meet in the market place. Just look for the one-eyed camel driver named Mohammed. Of course he said the name Mohammed and everyone in the market turned and said 'yes.'

For a man that has traveled in the diplomatic circles, Atia was a real whiner. He had been working on his flat for five years, and couldn't get this, or that was delayed. Of course he couldn't be seen at certain places with me, since I was a foreigner. Diplomats and Military men cannot be married to foreigners and stay with the Egyptian government. I guess they think we are all spies. So, I assume it was okay to be seen with me if there was a chance for him to get a free lay, which was probably why he was in such a hurry to get his flat finished. Mustafa wouldn't let him come up the stairs at my place, no matter how much he yelled about being a diplomat. It was nice having someone watch over you.

Now I had the best of all the worlds. The oil men had a flat with a washer and dryer which I used, an Egyptian diplomat that played bridge and could take me to seedy Egyptian clubs, a place to stay and swim on the weekends, and intellectual people to have a great conversation with from the embassies.

Everyone seems to know your business before you do. George Saad in the bridge club knew I wasn't seeing Atia, and started his move. Only his was more indirect. He knew I was working with computers and had been asking where I might purchase some part that would take me weeks to order through the Embassy. He had a grandson very good with computers. He would bring him by and see if he could help. Actually, he turned out to be a wonderful resource. There are no phone books, so if you try to purchase something, you have to run from store to store, and usually they don't have it. He found it for me right away. After that, I took tea with his daughter and her husband at their home. A delightful family, which now I was included in.

He knew the building in Garden City where the Library of Congress was located. He use to play bridge there with King Farouk on weekends. He was a Coptic, not Moslem, which was very unusual for his rank of General.

The Coptic church is based upon the teachings of St. Mark, who brought Christianity to Egypt in 50 AD. There are many sights in Egypt where the Holy family had taken shelter and refuge fleeing Judea and King Herod.

He was in the Army when Gamal Abdul Nasser was going to overthrow the King. General Nasser had asked him if he would be with them when they took over the Government. He said he couldn't do that, as he was friends with the King and would be playing poker with him that night. However, he would not say or do anything to interfere.

After the coup George was thrown in jail for about six months. Now in Egypt there's really no shame to going to prison, it's more like a badge of honor. Even now appointees to positions are thrown in jail when the government doesn't like what they do. I met the Minister of Culture, and he was thrown in jail for an art exhibit the government didn't like.

George had to leave the service, and the best I can figure out, he was selling military equipment to someone. He was and older, gentle man, until it came to bridge. You didn't want to be on the side of a bad bid with him. He'd asked me to marry him. By now I have had about 10 proposals, but his was really sincere. There was a bit of a problem with him being Coptic. He was a divorcee, and they can't remarry. So he was willing to become a Moslem so he could marry me. Actually that was a big thing, as he never converted to stay in the service during Nasser's time. No to Nasser, yes to Natasha. Let's face it, who wouldn't be getting puffed up with ten proposals, a party every night, a different date each week-end. Some might be imagining I was feeling 'is that all there is, and something is missing'. Not yet. After the cancer I said I was going to live every moment, and that's where I was at this stage of my life.

Each weekend Vern would send his driver with flowers and candy, wanting me to return for the parties. He realized now I was an intellectual woman, and not just one of those party girls. Please come. I PROMISE you I will be a perfect gentleman. The Queen's messenger at your service. One week-end I had to reply. He had sent me a cartouche with my name on it, which he told me he couldn't return. I decided to go out and found them at the pool. It looked like it was about time for their flop over, they were getting pretty red. Actually Vern was setting by himself, had his glasses on, and reading some work papers. When I approached, I found out he was sober!

He told me how nice it was to see me, and he'd love to just have a simple meal and be able to talk like an adult with me. They we building a oil facility and like everyone else in Egypt, was behind schedule. He'd just received some software that cost about $50,000 on critical path scheduling. He had been reading the instructions for two days, and still couldn't figure it out. I told him I'd studied it in Business School and would take a look at it. We spent the afternoon having a beautiful quiet lunch with all the gang passed out for their nap. He was a totally different person when he wasn't drinking. Now where have you heard that before?

I had the most exciting evening, as he took me to the main-frame and showed me the software. This was exciting to me, as it was cutting edge technology at that time. Doesn't take much to please me! He was so happy to have someone explain how it worked. We went to the movie and when we saw all the gang getting ready to party again, decided to have dinner in his suite.

"When you live and work overseas, your form your own family, usually of your workers. You numb yourself to the real world by drinking and partying. I'm not a spring chicken, I shouldn't be burning the candle at both ends. I knew when you ran off, I'd lost all concept of being a gentleman. I miss being around a lady and acting like a gentleman again. I hope we'll be seeing more of each other, on what ever level you wish" his eyes were looking down, he really did feel bad. Later on I found out he had been ban from the Queens Birthday party, which is the big gala for the British Embassy. It had to do with the swimming pool, don't ask.

He showered while we waited for dinner to arrive. When he returned, he was wearing Aramis. This was like catnip to me. I started thinking about how I had bonded with groups to form a family, and started reminiscing about a normal life. He was nice and tan, had silver hair, and a really nice body. We sat on the balcony and enjoyed the evening breeze. He asked me what I wanted to do next, and I said I'd like to study the software some more. We went to the mainframe and I stood behind him, showing him how to get from one menu to the next. Everyone has there own turn on, I guess mine must be a mixture of software and Aramis. He had that lovely bed in the suite, and we ended up on the hard wooden floor without bedding or pillow. Well, he did say the decision would be mine.

One of the crazy ex-pats from the oil group was going to Jordan, did anyone want to go? In a normal situation, this would sound crazy, but nothing was normal about living in Egypt. I'd never been there, so I said I'd go. Wild Bruce pulled me over and said, "He's safe, he's gay, but he's wrecked three vehicles already. Check whose going to drive before you go." He said, "no problem, the Company has him a driver now."

I hadn't had time to do much traveling yet, so this would be fun. We were going to Petra, Jordan, a city carved into the rocks. That's where Indiana Jones was filmed when they found the treasurer. They were just opening a new ferry service from Nuweib to Aqaba, and we could be one of the first to cross.

LUTISHA TESAREK

We would drive the first night to St. Catherine's Monastery built around the burning bush, where Moses received the Ten Commandments. The drive started off okay, only Harry kicked his driver out at the edge of town and took over the driving. How bad could he be? The Egyptians drive at night with no lights, as it's impolite to shine the light in your eyes. They drive on both sides of the streets, even their one ways streets have three degrees. One is, well, if it's convent this is a one-way, then this is one-way all the time, and the third is absolutely one way, Allah will strike you down if you go up this street. They even drive on railroad tracks when the traffic is backed up. So how bad can Harry be?

Well, I found out how bad Harry can be. I must have wet my pants ten times. At least he left his lights on so they could see him coming. This of course caused a constant honking of horns to let him know they we're pleased with him. When we go to the desert it wasn't that bad as there wasn't much traffic. We arrived late at the Monastery, after the gates had been locked. Harry's mentality was baksheesh works for everything, which was usually true. He apparently had been here before as he knew the gateman's name. They did the five minute introduction, he gave him a gift and baksheesh, and he opened the door, motioning to us to be quiet.

Apparently when the gates are locked, no one is allowed in. I noticed he had to give baksheesh three different times. He'd told him I was his sister, so we would be staying in the same room. I was hoping Wild Bruce knew what he was talking about when he said he was gay. I'd hate to have to walk back from the middle of the desert. His only interest was sleep. Tomorrow was another long drive. There was no moon so it was pitch black,

THE FINAL COMMANDMENTS

you couldn't see a thing. We were told not to turn the lights on so they wouldn't know we came in after the gate had been sealed. It was too cold to take a shower, as there was no heat in the room. When the sun goes down, the temperature can go to freezing in the desert. Harry loved the fresh air and opened the windows, making it really cold.

Next morning we had breakfast with a Monk Arsenios, whom Harry had brought some brandy for. He was very pleased to see me, and meet another one of Harry's sisters. We both laughed, and both knew it was a lie. I hope he didn't think I slept with him! But why should I care what he thought, I would never see him again.

Monk Arsenios gave me some history of the Monastery. It was Greek Orthodox, built around the burning bush to protect it. It's the only Monastery that has never been conquered, and has the richest icon collection in the world. Its library is second in importance only to that of the Vatican, in both number and value of manuscripts. It's first building was in 330 AD, then from 527 to 565 AD they completed the great walled monastery fortress. The rock wall is six to nine feet thick, and use to not be even a door. They used a basket to bring up the people.

I must say the first time I went out the gate and actually saw the Monastery, it was a mystical experience. Just the though that I could be standing in the same spot that Moses had stood made me start to pay attention to historical matters.

Monk Arsenios was going to give us a special tour, especially when he found out I was a librarian. Harry would have nothing to do with it, we were on a tight schedule and had to leave. The Monk smiled and said on my next visit I will show you things only a few are privileged to see. We thanked him for his hospitality and hoped in the car. He smiled a waved, and said "I'll be expecting you. You are a chosen one." I was trying to remember that phrase about being a chosen one. I'd heard it someplace. He was waving, smiling, and saying, till the next time. Yea, like I'm going to come 350 miles in the middle of the desert for a weekend when I could be swimming at the el Salam Hyatt Hotel. I waved and smiled back.

Now we were running into traffic on the highway. Apparently President Mubarak plus other important people were at the opening of the ferry and were on their way back. When we arrived at Nuweiba there was a security problem, we couldn't go for another three hours. It was right on the boarder of Israel, so we went over to a five star hotel in Taba and had an ice cream Sunday. It felt good to be someplace where there was ice and nice clean areas. Later on with the Peace Accord Israel would have to give this beautiful hotel to Egypt. Many years later the hotel would be hit by terrorist bombs any many people killed.

There was one thing baksheesh couldn't take care of, Harry couldn't take the car on the ferry. This means we'll have to stay an extra night waiting for transportation on the other side. We ended up on a busload of migrant workers, and I was the only woman.

I had seen pictures of Petra, the treasure of ancient world, which is hidden, behind the mountains. The rock-carved rose colored Petra is full of mysterious charm, and considered the most famous site in Jordan. It is between Amman, the capitol, and the seaport of Aqaba. As we approached through the mile long, cool, narrow gorge with steeply rising sides that all but obliterate the sun, I could understand how it had been hidden from the world for so many centuries. Suddenly the gorge opens into a natural square with the carved city of Petra looming above you.

Petra had flourished for over 400 years around the time of Rome and Christ, until it was occupied by the Roman legion of the Emperor in 106 AD. Located at the crossroads of the flourishing overland caravan trade routes, Petra prospered as the capital of the Nabataean empire from 400 BC to AD 106. The Nabataeans engineered a system of pipes, tunnels, and channels that carried drinking water into the city and reduced flash floods. When the Romans annexed Petra in AD 106, it's commercial hub slowly deteriorated. By the end of the Byzantine Empire, AD 700, the hydraulic system had deteriorated to near ruins. Petra then disappeared from most maps and was only known through ancient lore. The Bedouin's protected it and kept outsiders away, only Muslim were allowed in. In 1812 a Swiss traveler disguised himself as a Muslim trader and entered Petra, then preceded to tell the secret to the outside world.

We met the Bedouin tribe that use to live in the caves. The government of Jordan discovered this would be a nice tourist attraction, and built them apartments, which they wouldn't live in. They put up tents the distance the government told them they had to be away from Petra. Of course Mohammed was the leader, and he had a son named, you guessed it, Mohammed. The son Mohammed had a blonde haired British woman he was married to hanging on to two of their children. That's a bit too meshed in the culture for me. The eldest Mohammed started bargaining with my "brother" for my hand in marriage. Two camels were a good price. I wouldn't have to live in the tent with the other wives, I could live in the apartments the government had built. It would be almost like home. He had never offered this much to anyone before, so this was a great honor for me. He liked my blonde hair and blue eyes, a great advantage in the desert. His son had a blonde haired wife, and it just wasn't right for the father not to have one. I bet if Harry could have gotten the camels back, I'd be setting in the desert being Mrs. Mohammed IV.

The trip back on the ferry was uneventful. Harry told me just to relax, go to sleep and we'd be back in Cairo in no time. Yea, like I would sleep with him driving. I know why they call those handles in the cars sissy sticks. He said he'd brought two big containers of gas so we wouldn't have to stop at the first station. Well, that REALLY made me feel secure, him driving 120 miles an hour and some camel wandering on the road with 20 gallons of gas on my rear. If we made it back safely, the Monastery and Petra would be worth the other hardships.

Just when you think it can't get any worse, I woke up to this terrible grinding noise. I looked up and the front of the car was all smoke. I said, "Aren't you going to stop." No, if he stopped he'd never get it started again. Maybe it just needs oil. He forgot to bring oil, only gas. Maybe water, forgot water, only gas. Now I know why they call him Crazy Harry. I've got to start paying more attention to people's nicknames, there's a reason for them.

Finally the car just stopped. There we were, hundreds of miles from nowhere, in the desert, oh we had gas, but did we have water, or oil? Apparently he was a little weak on the details. I'd hate to think of the project he's working on.

There are certain unspoken rules by the Bedouins in the desert. Anything that doesn't move belongs to them. All of a sudden we are surrounded by a complete tribe of Bedouin's asking us how they could help. Come with us to there camp and relax until morning. We both knew the minute we left the car it would disappear. We thanked them and told them we had a group right behind us that would be able to help. Mohammed knows much about cars, come to our camp and he'll fix it for you. Yea, I'm sure Mohammed has a lot of practice working on those camels, I thought to myself. Harry was in his negotiating stage, what a sweet guy. He'd just given them all the things I'd bought in Petra for their wives. I wonder when he was going to give away is stuff.

"Harry, listen, I hear something!" You couldn't see anything as they drive with their lights off. Then the noise got louder and louder, it sounded like a military convoy. Actually, that's what it turned out to be. It was the last of the security team coming home from the celebration. Harry got out and flagged them down. He was in his element now, as these poor guys got about $10 a month, and baksheesh went a long way. He wanted them to pull the car back to Cairo for him. No, they couldn't do that without there Commanders permission. No amount of baksheesh could make them let go of their fear of the Commander.

Then, the solution arrived. Some poor truck driver was hauling a load to Cairo. He was flagged down and ordered to pull the car for Harry. He didn't want to do it, but wasn't given a choice. I wanted to set up front in the truck and away from Harry. No, no! This scared him. To be alone with a woman could get him in trouble. I told him I'd get in back again before we reached the checkpoint.

Harry was left in back with a flashlight in case the truck had to stop and he had to put on his brakes. I'd glance back every so often and see this little light and laughed to myself. I'm sure he hadn't gone this slowly since he'd been in Egypt. The next time I glanced back there was no light. The truck driver slammed on the breaks so fast I hit the dashboard. His concern was not for Harry, but for being alone with a woman! He really turned that big truck around fast, he even turned on his lights. When we got back to the car, it was surrounded by another Bedouin tribe. Harry was very happy to see us. I think he finally had to get into his stash.

The rope had broken and was really short now. Harry only had about six feet between him and the truck. I had no pity for him, and could just imagine him slumped over the steering wheel getting as close as he could to the windshield to see how close he was to the truck.

We made it to the Suez Canal around 2 A.M. We couldn't even pay the truckers duty fee, we'd given all our money as baksheesh to the military and Bedouins. Actually crossing under Suez in the tunnel is like going to another country. It's passports, papers, etc. Harry was going to leave the car there and have the company pick it up in a few days. Of course they'd need a 'fee' to leave it there. Harry started yelling he didn't have any baksheesh left. They yelled back, it's not baksheesh, it's a ligament fee for parking. Now the guards were going to use all their bureaucracy power to find something wrong with the car to charge him more. They knew all foreigners were rich and always carried lots of money hidden on them. Wasn't the car a Mercedes? That means big money.

They had agreed to let the truck driver go on, we could get a taxi later on. Open the truck, one of them yelled at Harry. He opened the trunk and went over to get a soda. One of the guards started yelling, for the others to come. I thought, they must have found their broken taillight they were looking for. Two of them came running back to us with pointed guns. Another ran to the truck and pulled the truck driver out of the truck and had him on the ground. This was getting scary, your dealing with loaded guns pointed at you. You could just disappear and no one would know where. All I could think of is you need to let them know you can get money to them.

The excitement was over the 20 gallons of gas in the trunk. Harry had explained he'd taken it so he wouldn't run out in the desert. They had lined us up in a row with our hands over our head. I needed to get to a phone. I had also dated General Mustafa Salah, the personal bodyguard for President Mubarak. I had his private phone number with me, thank heaven.

I took my American Passport and told them I worked at the Embassy and wanted to call there. The phone was not working. I know it was, because I just saw them use it. Usually an American Passport and the Embassy will bring some reaction, but nothing. Okay, I'd play my trump card, the Generals name and number. I told them to call General right now, and gave him the private number. "The General will not help you in this matter, Madam" he said is a cold voice and his black eyes burned right through mine.

I was getting scared now, they apparently were so mad at Harry that nothing, not even baksheesh, was going to work. I started thinking about never seeing my children again, and started crying. Then I heard them speaking anxiously to each other. Then I remembered the equalizer. They can't take a woman crying! Also what was the truck driver so scared of? Being alone with a woman! Then I really stared crying, with tears running down my face. "halal, halal" I yelled. I am the only woman here with all of you men. You cannot keep me here. People know I've been here. Military men helped tie the car to the truck. You have registered the truck in your records. They can trace me to here. If you do not release us this very moment, I will tell them you did horrible things to me.

That did it, they took our addresses in case they wanted to question us again, and let us go. I felt so sorry for the truck driver. He was just doing us a favor, and ended up almost in jail.

The next day when I went to work I realized what was happening, and how lucky we were to actually get out. There is no diplomatic relations with Libya, Egypt or the United States. The rumor was Kadafi from Libya was going to blow up the Suez Canal, and here we are with 20 gallons of gas in our car. I didn't see wild Harry at any of the parties. I assume four cars being wrecked were enough for his company.

8

TROUBLE IN EGYPT – COUP AND HIJACKING

One night I was woke by the phone and it was Vern. He sounded very anxious and told me not to go out tonight for any reason, there was trouble on the streets. I asked him how bad it was and he said they'd put him on alert. The executives had what they called an S.O.S. card. Corporations have a guarantee if there's any trouble they'll get them out of the country, even if it's by camel. Vern advised me tomorrow when I go out be sure and take my valuables and plenty of cash in case I can't get back to my flat. I called the Marines after he hung up and asked if they knew of any trouble. I figured if anyone would know what was going on, it would be the Embassy. They had just heard there was some sort of riot out by the Pyramids. Food was subsidized and every time bread went up a piaster they would riot. That was a long way from where I lived, so I was going to be like Scarlet and worry about it tomorrow.

I did call my Field Director, as he had two young children he sent to school. I suggested he didn't send them to school tomorrow. He just laughed at me, and said if there were any trouble the Embassy would let him know. When I thought about it, I felt foolish. He was on the big cheese list, and I was just a Consultant, not in the loop. He knew the crowd I ran with and wouldn't be impressed with any information they gave me.

I went to work the next day and was in a meeting when the secretary Mona came running through yelling, "Maadi is burning, Maadi is burning!" Maadi is a town about 20 miles away where she lived, and where the private school for the American children was. The Field Director looked at me in shock. How the hell could I know this when the Embassy didn't even know? Finally there was a call from Security telling everyone they had one hour to get home and off the streets or the regular police might shoot them. Get whatever food supplies you can and don't come out of your flat until you're told it's okay.

The little information we got was a certain branch of the police had a coup to take over the government. This was the branch that guarded the hotels and embassies, and had charge of the Armory and tanks! They had released prisoners and were burning down the buildings.

Zamalek was an island, and I recall Vern warning me it would be a bad place to be as they could block all the bridges and you couldn't get out. Then I remember one of the regulars at the bar bragging about how he could get a plane if they ever needed to get out real fast, but no gas. The other one replied

THE FINAL COMMANDMENTS

hell I can get the gas. One of them was from Texas and he'd said to me, "Missy, if we ever have to get out of this hell hole fast, you come with us, old Tex will get you out." The two Americans with brief cases handcuffed to their wrist had been bragging about how one's missiles could shoot down anything in the sky. The other yelled back, "Can't get me, because MY plane is off the radar screen!" Finally two oversized men when microphones in there ear came and dragged them off before they gave away too many secrets.

I kept trying to get a taxi, yelling Zamalak, but they knew they could get on the island but maybe not be able to get off. When they'd say no, no, I'd ask them where they were going. "I've got to get home to my family in Heliopolis" the driver said as I ran along side the taxi. I hopped in and say, just take me to the El Salam Hotel, it's on your way. La, la!! Yes, here's 50 pounds! Mind you, that would be his regular profit for a month! "Get down, get gown" he yelled to me as two police-men came by. I knew enough Arabic to understand they were telling him to get off the streets. He told them he was headed home now. I felt the taxi go fast, then come to an screeching halt. Every horn was honking, everyone was yelling at the top of their voices. It seemed like an eternity, then I heard the car stop as something hit it. It was the tip of a policeman's gun hitting the door. I could just understand bits and pieces of the conversation. The driver told the policeman I was sick and he was trying to get rid of me by dumping me at the nearest hotel so he wouldn't be responsible, the El Salam was just around the corner. "Good thinking", the policeman replied.

When we got to the hotel there were tanks all around it. I forgot the ones that did the coup were in charge of the tanks.

The man jumped off the tank and in front of the taxi. He pointed the gun right at the taxi driver. I swore this wasn't going to be another truck driver incident. I jumped out of the taxi and yelled "halal" at the top of my voice. The solder was in shock at a woman doing this. I told the taxi to go on, and pushed the gun away from the taxi. I knew about 20 Arabic words, and was yelling them at the solder. Then, I just turned, straightened my hair, and walked toward the hotel, not knowing if I was going to get a bullet in the back. I saw Mustafa running towards me, greeting me, saying they are so happy that their honored guest found their way back in these troubled times. He sent me in and gave baksheesh to the solder.

If I ever felt like a drink, this was it. My knees were shaking at the thought of what would have happened if Mustafa hadn't come to get me.

It was like going into the twilight zone. You would never know there were tanks surrounding the hotel, everything was normal inside. All the gang was at the pool, their only concern was that they'd run out of Stella beer before this thing was over.

Apparently the hotels were to be the oasis for the duration. You couldn't go out, but you were safe inside. I think Mustafa the Manager had made an agreement with the solders giving them meals and baksheesh. Apparently other companies had figured this out, for now we had Germans, Italians, Indians, and the American Companies had sent the staff that lived in flats.

It turned out to be almost an international dispute every day. The Germans were really angry because the British had bought up all the Stella Beer ahead of time. Now it became a ritual for each county to plant there flag by the umbrella and if ANYONE toughed it there would be a fight. That wasn't enough, they started singing their national anthem as loud as possible while waving the flag. Now the arguments weren't missiles against planes, but country against country. Why didn't these guys just settle this by pulling out their willies and whoever had the longest was the winner.

General Dynamics and Teledyne Brown Engineering, two large contract companies from the United States, had pulled their people in also. This is the first time I had seen them. Most high profile companies don't allow their employees to be out in public for security reasons.

It was like a week on holiday. The hotel put on extra movies, and had special entertainment each night. It reminded me of the story Tomaso told of when they were stranded in South American during a coup and couldn't get back to the ship. They were held up in a brothel for a week and had it put on their charge card. The company had to pay the charge, as they couldn't get back to the ship.

I got acquainted with some of the Americans. Apparently not everyone likes to drink as much as our crowd. I was setting having tea by myself and they asked if I wanted to set with them. It was a nice change from the national anthem contest at the pool. These were top level men I could tell. They felt more comfortable when they found out I worked at the embassy. I guess everyone is a potential spy. However, it wasn't until one of them had excused himself to make a call and came back later that we talked about things other than the coup. I assumed they had went to their sources, as none of the local phones were working. They though it strange an American being protected by the British and not the embassy. I told them I was under contract from Washington, D.C., and the embassy had no responsibility for me. Yes, they were probably in the same situation, Americans, but on your own.

One of the gentlemen with General Dynamics was a retired Admiral, and the project had something to do with the F-16. He would be one of the 17 men hijacked on TWA and flown to Lebanon. I think they were held for about two weeks. I remember seeing in Time Magazine where they profiled all the men. It said he worked for General Dynamics, but that he was working on "low income housing in the desert'. I'm sure he wouldn't be here today if they connected him to the F-16.

The other group was tearing apart Russian Missiles to see if the United States could learn something from their technology.

During that week I did some sole searching. Was this really what I meant when I said live every day to the fullest. I found myself wanting more quiet time. Too much excitement can be boring also.

My crazy roommate from Hawaii came over to spend a month with me. She lives in California now, and had the summer off, as she was a school librarian. We meet her at the airport, and there she is in shorts! We really enjoyed our shopping time together, as she was a vegetarian and there was wonderful fruits and vegetables at the market. Aziz, the maid, just couldn't believe we wanted to do our own shopping. Usually foreigners don't go out and let the maid do all the shopping. Actually it worked out cheaper. By the time Kimberly asked all these questions, how fresh, where was it grown, did they use pesticides, they practically gave it to us.

She traveled to Upper Egypt by herself, and we decided to go to the Sinai together. She was a scuba diver, and Ras Mohamed was one of the most beautiful spots on earth for diving. We

THE FINAL COMMANDMENTS

took my neighbor Nina, who was from Germany and taught piano. She also wanted to go to St. Catherine Monastery. I was between contracts and said we could all go together. We were just going for two days, and I took only one change of clothing. I remembered Crazy Harry saying the Monks have no money, and was really pleased when someone brought them a gift. I got a bottle of brandy for Monk Arsenios. He did say I was coming back, didn't he?

The bus ride was straight out of hell. Nina spoke Arabic and was yelling at them all night. Everyone was a chain smoker, and the video was blasting for 18 hours in Arabic so loud you couldn't think. You prayed you didn't have to go to the bathroom, as it's a filthy hole in the floor, and apparently no one can hit the mark. You know you've lived in Egypt too long when you start thinking Crazy Harry would be better transportation.

It was a beautiful late afternoon, as we arrived passing small groups of Bedouin's in colorful garb traveling on camel. The sunset was breathtaking. The air was so clear and fresh. Just imagine stepping out of a smoked filled, noisy, crowded, smelly bus onto the sand where Moses walked. There is no pollution or noise, just the whisper of the wind.

We brought our own food, as there was a community kitchen where we could cook. While we were cooking a note came from Monk Arsenios. Would we join the Monks for tea tonight? As I said, everyone knows your business in Egypt before you do. I assume the Bedouin guard remembered me

The Bedouin tribe that guards the Monastery are Moslem, and have guarded it for centuries. They're like an extended family. Although their not highly educated, many of them speak at least three languages.

We washed up as best we could for our tea. I know some of the smell from the bus must still be on me. It is a very high honor to be invited to tea I found out later on. It's usually just Ambassadors, United Nations, and high-ranking officials.

The monks were very pleased with the Brandy, and even more pleased when we said we didn't drink. That means they didn't have to open it now, and could take just little sips now and then to make it last longer. There were 17 monks living at the Monastery, most of them from Greece. There was one from Australia, a couple from Europe, and one from Germany. Nina took him on in her brash way about where he was from and all his history. Then the conversation became quiet when one of the monks from Europe stated he'd been in a German prisoner of war camp during World War II.

To break the silence the Arch Bishop mentioned how much they appreciated the Library of Congress for microfilming much of their archived material. In 1955 the Library of Congress microfilmed most of their manuscripts. The librarian started telling us about his library, the most unique library in the world. Two-thirds are in Greek, while the rest are in Arabic, Syriac, Georgian, Armenian, Coptic, Ethiopian and Slavonic. It contains historical documents bearing the gold or lead seals of Emperors Patriarchs, Bishops and Turkish Sultans. This included Mohammed's Proclamation of Protection, and Napoleon's Declaration of Protection. Apart from its valuable manuscripts, it also contains some 5,000 books, some of them produced in the first decades after the invention of print.

THE FINAL COMMANDMENTS

The most important volume is the Codex Syriacus from the 5th Century. This oldest translation of the gospels was discovered only in 1892. The Monastery legally owns the bible. It was borrowed in 1865 by a German scholar on behalf of the Russian Czar for research and never returned. In 1933 the British Museum purchased it from the Soviets. The British Museum refuses to return it, even after the Monastery offered to reimburse them for the bible.

Their icon collection consists of 2,000, with twelve of the rarest and oldest icons of the 6th century. You could tell he was very proud of the collection.

He asked me if I was doing more microfilming with the Library of Congress. I explained my project consisted of using computers to catalog and keep records for billing and shipping of the collections for the Middle East and North Africa. Many academic and large libraries around the world have no way to purchase books printed in Egypt for research. There is no system for book buyers in place. The Library of Congress purchases the books and ships them around the world at cost for the academic community. My program has combined the cataloging information in one place, and then each department takes the information they need, and doesn't have to type it again. We had 88 separate forms to be filled out, now it is down to 15.

The Arch Bishop returned to the subject of computers. He was lost with this new computer technology. He heard they were wonderful, but didn't understand anything about them. In fact, he stated, we have two computers the University of Greece sent us, and we don't know what to do with them. I told him I'd be glad to set them up for the Monastery, and do training if they so desired.

That would be wonderful, could I stay and do it this time? He was leaving for Germany tomorrow, but I would be there guest and stay as long as I needed.

They didn't have electricity until after the 1967 war between Egypt and Israel. When Israel occupied the Sinai they installed two large generators for the Monastery. They only turn them on one hour at night, but the Archbishop would make arrangements for them to be on when I needed electricity.

Kimberly and I got up about 2 A.M. to climb the mountain where Moses received the 10 Commandments. You either go at sunrise or sunset. If you go at sunset, you must stay overnight as it's too dangerous to come back down at night. There was no moon, so it was pitch black for our climb. We were walking in the dark and all of a sudden we heard out of the shadows a soft voice repeating, "Want a camel? Want a camel? I'll give you a good price." I guess no matter where you are, they will be vendors. He assured us he could take clear to the top, for the best price. It's a good thing we didn't take his offer, the camels can go only about two miles and then you're on your own. If there hadn't been other people we never would have found our way. It was so dark. Much of it was like rock climbing, grabbing corners of the rock and pulling yourself up. The closer you got to the top, the more people just seemed to appear. Then you could hear the mummer of voices, letting you know you were getting closer.

It was still dark when we arrived, and the atmosphere was like an international bazaar. There must have been twenty different nationalities. There was a small Bedouin serving tea. At least he didn't have competition up here. This meant his water and other supplies had to be hauled up. If I heard anyone com-

THE FINAL COMMANDMENTS

plaining about the price, I personally would throw them off the mountain. Of course there is always that one American that keeps our reputation as spoiled with no manners. Here's this poor little man doing the best he can to serve all these people and the American steps up and asks, "Got any hot chocolate?" I suppose he thought he was at the Russian Tea Room back in New York.

As the sun started to rise, we all remembered what we were here for, and all conversations stopped. I calm came over all, and breathed in the most beautiful sunrise I have ever seen. It cast shadows over the mountains and the colors just kept changing with every movement of the sun. I felt a universal peace being gathered at this sacred place with these people from around the world. My heart felt so full, I wanted this feeling for the entire world, for the resources of the world to be spent for the betterment of man, instead of tearing the world apart with destructive confrontations.

Kimberly and I started making up our Ten Commandments for librarians to leave on the mountain. About the only one I can remember is "Thou shall not dog ear pages of library books." We walked back down with two young priests from Europe.

Nina and Kimberly went on to Ras Mohammed and I stayed behind. I thought it would only be a few days. The Law of Divine order; there are no accidents, your energy, translated in thoughts and feelings cause all your experiences.

Suliman, who was the Monks cook, would cook for me. Monk Arsenios was the Secretary for the Archbishop, so he would be my contact. The computers were IBM, with one disk of DOS, two were missing, a word processor, and a Greek program. We had a 'topping off' party for the computers when they were turned on, and Monk Arsenios and I gave them names.

What started out to be a few days, ended up being over a month. I was limited to about two hours of electricity, and Monk Arsenios had his regular duties, plus Vespers in the afternoon when everything came to a standstill. I would do what I called my lizard time, I'd go lay on the rocks in the sun. I must say it was the most peaceful time I have ever known. I kept thinking to myself, every time I would walk, "this could be the exact steps that Moses took." In this location and atmosphere you couldn't help but start thinking on a spiritual level.

Growing up of course you go to church, it's part of the curriculum. I was raised hard shell Southern Baptist when I was younger. Then when I was married and with young children in California, it was the First Baptist Church. We were the typical young family in church. He was a Deacon, I taught Sunday school and President of the Women's Missionary Society. The children were baptized and we attended potlucks. But when my mother died I was very angry with God. How could he let this happen? It's really funny the things we will blame on God.

Each one of the Monks had a cat that would follow him around. It was a relationship like a dog, I've never seen cats follow people around. They would also have small goats as pets. The older Monks didn't like the idea of me being there. A woman shouldn't be in the Monastery.

I was to instruct Monk Arsenios on the computers, so we spent the evenings together while the electricity was on. He would be talking to me about my soul and always say, "how is your material life working for you?" He kept asking when I was going to be ready to fulfill my obligation on earth. Instead of me educating him, he was educating me. I told him I didn't understand what he was saying.

This is when he started my many lessons. The power of words, especially the I AM, the house of hidden knowledge, sent to Egypt from Atlantis over 10,500 years ago with the Final Commandments consisting of the Universal Laws based on energy, and the Akashic records where all information is stored.

A new scientific technique dealing with DNA could connect people for thousand of years with just a sample of skin or hair. Jesus left samples in the Alexandria Library Archives for future generations in case there were false claims against him. The first challenge will come with the Shroud of Turin. Some microbiologist believe the cloth is covered with living "bioplastic" coating of bacteria and fungi. They believe the blood on the shroud is ancient and contains XY chromosomes, which establishes it as human and male. The DNA chain is very long, and they are able to identify very small sectors representing individual characteristics which can ultimately enable them to identify the individual from whom they derive. I time might come when proof of who Jesus really was will have to be revealed to keep people in power from distorting the truth about Jesus to control the masses. At that time, the chosen people will have to decide rather to release this information or not.

This information was too technical for me. I just wanted to live my life, be a good human being, and help other people however I can. I wanted to stay away from religion.

I was given references and books I should read. It seems I just graduated, and now he wants me to start all over again!

The Monastery was to be locked each night at 9 P.M. with only the Monks being inside. The key man was named Mohammed (surprise) and yes, weighed about 90 pounds and 100 years old. He fell asleep one night and didn't wake up to 11 P.M. He was really scared that a woman was inside the Monastery and came running with horror in his voice shouting, "Madam teacher, madam teacher, you must leave at once." The key to the gate was almost as tall as he was, probably weighted 30 pounds, and he was dragging it behind him.

It wasn't that we did anything wrong, we were just talking. Now the Monks were really upset. I had broken a rule, not being out by a given time. I was not aware of the time, no one had told me. I felt very uncomfortable now, I knew some of them didn't want me there. When I found out some of them were going to their Abbey in Cairo I asked if I could ride with them.

Monk Arsenios was very disappointed I was leaving. I don't know if they get so many points for saving sinners, but he defiantly was after my sole. Natasha, you must come back. You're not aware of it yet, you have much studying yet, and there is a purpose for you on earth. He was scaring me now, I'd stayed away from religion since my mother died.

We traveled at night to avoid the terrible heat of the desert. There were three monks and myself, in a Mercedes given to them by French President Meterand.

I thought back over my time at the Monastery. I had actually met more dignitaries there in one month than my whole life combined. All the special guests would have tea with the Monks at night. The Ambassador from Britain came with the United Nations peacekeepers. They lived at Sharm el Sheikh and came twice a year to clean up the trash tourist left. The peacekeepers would walk up Mt. Moses and collect the trash. Then a helicopter would pick it up. The Ambassadors wife from Sweden and two of her friends were there and we had some wonderful conversations. One of the ladies was an official judge for the Nobel Peace Prize. A scholar from Greece was writing a book on their icon collection. When she left the car was broken down and she had to ride on the tractor down to meet the bus. I helped her load her suitcases on.

Going through the checkpoint at the Suez Canal was relatively different than my first experience with Crazy Harry. We were treated like diplomats.

9

LEAVING EGYPT

Since returning from the Monastery I had continued my studies of the Alexandria Library and the Nag Hammadi Library. Earlier in my research I was given confidential information that when Jesus studied at the Alexandria Library, his DNA was left in the Hall of Records with the Universal Laws, which had been passed down over 10,500 years ago from Atlantis; even older than Moses Ten Commandments. Apparently their society was well advanced, as it has taken us over 2,000 years to 'discover' DNA. I had been working with an organization putting together documentation verifying Jesus time in Egypt, his true association with women in the church structure, and his initiation at Heliopolis and at the Pyramids, which transformed him to the Christ.

THE FINAL COMMANDMENTS

The Nag Hammadi Library has earned quite a reputation. From its discovery it has been surrounded by extremism, intrigue and mystery. It has to translate, do to the fact there are only about 100 people who knows the Coptic language. In 1945 there was the discovery of the large jug containing the codices by one of two peasant brothers who had come to collect nitrate-laden rocks for fertilizer at the base of large cliffs flanking the Nile river valley. Surrounding the discovery of the documents was ignorance and greed. Those codices that were not burned found their way into various hands, including those of a priest, the priest's brother who taught English on an itinerary circuit, illiterate Muslims, a gold merchant, a grain merchant, a one-eyed outlaw who acquired most of them, a Belgian antiquities dealer and even the Jung Institute in Switzerland. Now, all remaining codices are conserved in the Coptic Museum in Cairo. Many of these are fruitlessly fragmentary. Nevertheless, about 30 fundamentally complete passages (called tractates) have survived their ordeal out of the jug. All the tractates had been translated from Greek into Coptic, which is the hieroglyphic language of ancient Egypt written with the Greek alphabet. They were not written for everyone, since few could read.

Most but not all of the tractates have been described as Gnostic writings from the early centuries after the death of Jesus Christ. Many contain quotations of Jesus. Some contain references to the Bible as well as extensive quotations from it. One such is the Gospel of the Egyptians, which contains marvelous passages attributed to Seth, a main character in the ancient Egyptian myth of Osiris.

I was working on my research when I heard a knock on the door. In Egypt this is a surprise, as no one gets past your bawwab. Finally after the third knock, I recognized Mustafa's voice apologizing and saying something about a message. I cracked the door and he slipped a note to me, again apologizing, making sure not to look at me.

It was from Vern. I hope he's not expecting me to go to a party now! I started reading it. I've never known him to be serious, but the tone of this letter was not the fun loving Vern I knew. It read, " Do NOT tell anyone about this note. As soon as you read it, burn it. There's a small hotel called the Windsor on Taha Hussein St. past Suny's Market. Go out like your going shopping, taking your shopping bag with you. Go slow and window shop on Hassen Sabri on your way there so it looks like you're out shopping. You might be followed. When you get to Suny's, back by the meat market is a side door you can go out. Slip out and come to the hotel through the back road. There's a side entrance, go to the second floor, room 12. Don't knock or turn the light on. I'll be waiting for you there."

I wondered if this was another of his surprise parties. He's always making up stories and then it ended up a party. What extremes that man goes to just for fun. I wonder if he ever had a serious bone in his body. I'd better throw good walking shoes in the shopping bag, no telling where we'll end up.

I started down Hassen Sabri window shopping. Egyptians love their nights, going up and down the streets, stopping at the juice stands. Only the men gather at coffee shops, so this leaves the street vendors along the way for the families. Of course there's the hotels, but a coffee and pastry would cost the average Egyptian a weeks pay. I passed a pharmacy store, and decided to go in. You can go into the pharmacies and get any medicine you want for about 10% what a prescription in America would cost. I always make sure I have a supply of penicillin pills. They cost about $2.50 for a weeks supply. Does that give you an idea of how much the pharmaceutical companies are making?

Suny's is a Supermarket run by Japanese, and the cleanest in Cairo. The vendors on the street hang meat on a hook outside. But there was something sweet about shopping on the street, knowing the vender, and having him put an extra piece of fruit in your bag.

I went into Suny's and started going up and down the isles. Eventually I went towards the meat market, and slipped out the back door. I followed the instructions and slipped into the hotel room. I stood there in the dark for what seemed to be an endless amount of time. I was waiting for the light to go on and 20 people to yell surprise, happy Sadie Hawkins Day or something like that. Suddenly I felt an arm around my waist and a hand over my mouth. It was Vern, signaling me to be quiet and follow him. We went into the closet and closed the door.

No more those laughing eyes, the Queen's messenger at your service. His face had a sadness I had never seen before. He had a small flashlight on. "Do you trust me Natasha? Because I'm going to tell you something for your own good, and your just going to have to believe me. I care for you more than you can imagine, and I'm putting myself at risk for doing this." He sounded like the burden of the world was on his shoulders. Puzzled, still wondering if this was one of his elaborate plots for a party, I asked, "Vern, what's wrong? Surely nothing could be this serious?"

He stated that I had to leave Egypt within a few days, as soon as possible. No one was to know, he had my ticket under an assumed name, and it would be changed at the last minute.

Because of the people I've been seen with, my life was in danger. I started laughing and felt relieved, this was another one of his stunts! He gripped my arm and spun me around, putting his hand over my mouth again. What is the matter with you woman, can you possibly be so naïve? Do you think you can run around with spies from the KGB, Egyptian government, gun runners, Special Forces and not be noticed? I'm not even for sure whose side you're on, or who put the contract out, but if you stay in Egypt you'll have an accident within a week!

"Vern, I'm tired of this game. In the first place, no one could be interested in any information I have. I'm a librarian, I'm cataloging books for crying out loud. I don't have any sort of security clearance. Someone wants me dead because I'm cataloging books?" Now it was my turn to end this charade. "As the old saying goes around the embassy, it's on a need to know basis, and I don't need to know."

He let out a sigh, and shook his head. "I guess you really are as trusting and naïve as you seem. This is the reason I care for you so much. You're the first person in my life for 20 years that has been sincere, and really care for other people. But you're out of your league here. You probably don't even know whom you've been running with. I'll say this only once, then I want you to forget it, and hope you don't run into these people ever again in your life.

You are living in the spy capitol of the Middle East. As the saying goes, a good spy is either someone that blends into the woodwork and you don't know they're there, or so visible you would never suspect them. The second one are how they have you pegged. No one can believe that you would associate with all these know people and not be in the same game. By the

THE FINAL COMMANDMENTS

way, Crazy Harry is back! He's KGB. He now has blonde hair
and a moustache, another job and name, but it's him. Didn't
it ever bother you when he had a rose lying on his front seat in
his car? That was his signal for a contact. That's why he had to
kick his driver out the time you went to Petra. He was probably
contacted at the first rest stop. Then your Coptic bridge partner that was throw in jail by Nasser during the revolution, he's
a common gun runner, playing both sides. Your other bridge
partner from the Egyptian State Department is similar to our
CIA. President Mubarak isn't too happy about you dating his
private bodyguard. When you called him at 3 A.M. from the
Suez Cannel, this sent alarm bells to every agency. You're probably not even aware of it, but one of the Americans you've been
seeing is Special Forces.

"You expect me to believe all of this?" I answered in anger. I
just wanted this past hour to disappear, and my life to go back
to fun and games. He took my hand and held it up to his lips.
I could feel a tear on my skin. Now I was scared. What he has
been saying is true, this isn't a game. This is crazy, no one has
every talked about anything that would be classified to me, but
someone thinks I'm a messenger or worse, a spy! Vern went on
to explain because I didn't drink and always had a clear head,
traveled through so many different circles of friends, I was a
natural to hear things, and perhaps pass the information on.
He looked into my eyes and realized I still couldn't believe this.
"Natasha, have you never wondered how I knew even before
your embassy about the coup? Do you really even know who I
am? Think about it, if you don't even know me, then perhaps
you have misjudged all these other people."

I started crying I didn't want to believe any of this. I just wanted my life back. "Natasha, you have friends that don't want to see you hurt, that's how I've found out about this. One is a CIA operative, posing as a businessman of course. I'm not saying how it knows you, but he knows you're in the wrong place at the wrong time. I don't know where he gets his information from, but it's always accurate. When they had the leader of the Achille Lauro Ship hijacking and murder on an Egyptian Plane to Tunisia, he had the real story. Arafat was going to have a speedy trial and the man was going to be hanged. He'd heard this on some high tech communication system. But you American's and your macho crap had to hijack the plane and he got away, to spend more years in terrorizing countries. If they had read and analyzed the information given to them by the CIA, they would have let well enough alone. They could see he was a threat to Arafat's power, so he was more than happy to be rid of him.

"Why are you doing this? If your in the game, it puts you in danger" I told him. "Yes, I know, but you might find another way for governments and leaders to run this world without blowing it up. At onetime I thought what I was doing was useful, but now I realize it's just causing hate and mistrust. Since you are such a trusting person, and believe only good in people, maybe you can find a better way. Maybe you will be one of the chosen to guide us away from total destruction." There was that phrases again, one of the chosen. Where had I heard that before?

Vern spent the next half-hour on the plan. He gave me the key to the room. Every time I went shopping I was to bring things I needed to get out of the country up here and leave it in the closet. When I left my apartment for the last time, I was to be carrying only my purse and shopping bag. Assume I was being watched, do not go down side streets, and always stay in busy areas. A phone call would come to me from my family, someone was sick, I had to leave right away, not knowing how long it would be. I would terminate my positions for family medical reasons. The date I purchased my ticket for would be two days after I left. I was to be ready to go on 12 hours notice. If need be, he'd use his S.O.S. card to get me out.

Leaving the hotel I went back in the back door of Suny's and finished my shopping. When I went out the front door again, I tried to see if there was anyone unusual around. I couldn't tell, the streets were always so full. I was wondering if this was just a bad dream. I actually pinched my self to see if I would come out of a nightmare.

I didn't sleep much that night. At about 10 A.M. the next day, a call was transferred to me. They said it was long distance from the United States. I wondered who could be calling me, it was so expensive. I heard an unfamiliar voice at the other end of the line. "Hello Mom, its Katie." I knew it wasn't Katie, but I had to remember what Vern said last night. "Is everything okay?" I asked. "Actually, I'm having trouble with my back again, and they might have to do some surgery. I don't know how long that would leave me off my feet. Do you have any vacation time coming?" I went along with this charade saying yes, I could be there probably within a week. Not to worry, that's what Mom's are for.

Whatever was going to happen, it looks like my days were numbered in the land of the Pharos. I had no choice now but to go along with Vern's plan. I went in a spoke with my Field Director and told him I had no idea how long I would be gone, but I would finish the documentation I was working on before I left. I worked late till 9 P.M. to finish my project. When I came out there was a taxi about half a block down the street. He followed me and asked if I wanted a taxi. La, la, shukran. "Madam, you are my last fare, only one pound to Zamalek." He insisted. That was it, how did he know I was going to Zamalek? I cut through a small path where a vehicle couldn't fit, and headed for the embassy. I went inside and asked the Marine if any vehicle was going to Zamalek, someone was harassing me. He got a vehicle to take me home.

I went about my business as routinely as possible. I received a call from a Tarek at the Travel desk. "Madam Natasha, I understand you are trying to get out of Cairo as quickly as possible because of a family illness. We have you wait listed for Friday, but a cancellation just came in for Wednesday's flight. You want me to put you on it?" I figured this was Vern's connection, I'd never heard of Tarek before. I asked him where Hassen was, he'd been working with me. "He had some family matters and will be off for a week" he replied. "I'll send a runner with you ticket. I got the same price for you, the agent at TWA is my cousin."

I had the ticket in my hand now, and Vern said I would be leaving a few days earlier than scheduled. He told me not to contact him, he'd be contacting me. I just did as he told me, take only my purse and a shopping bag. I started to walk up to Suny's thinking Vern might be at the room. When I came out there was a taxi there, said he'd been sent to take me to the airport. It must be Vern. So I got in the taxi.

We had started over the 26 of July Bridge and then turned left on the Cornish. "This isn't the way to the airport" I said.

THE FINAL COMMANDMENTS

"Yes, I know a shortcut, there's not as much traffic this way" he replied. I had lived here long enough to know this was going in the opposite direction. All of a sudden the taxi was hit from behind. Now we go into a ritual of who's to blame. There is no logic to this, but it actually works well, as it lets everyone get their frustration out without a actual blame being fixed to one person, saving face. I remember once being on a small bus that was just setting there waiting for a traffic light to change. The person in front had tried to get across the street illegally, and when he didn't make it, he backed into position, backing right into our bus. There is no way the man that hit the bus wasn't wrong. But everyone around gathers and takes sides. The two driver's circle each other like there in a cockfight, getting ready to charge. This is saving their honor. The people gathered around are yelling obscenities at the other side, telling them how much at fault they are. Then when the two in dispute start moving close enough for actual physical blows, people on each side grab their arms so they can't hit each other. Instead, the bystanders keep hurling insults at each other. This goes on for about fifteen minutes, and then everyone goes there own way. I was wondering if we had enough time for this song and dance before we made it to the airport.

At that moment someone grabbed my arm and yanked me out of the taxi. I'd never seen this done before! "Wait" I said. "I'm just the passenger." He whispered, "The Queen's Messenger at your service." The guy was from Vern. We got into another car and headed in the opposite direction. The two taxi drivers and the crowd were still doing their song and dance and hadn't even noticed I was gone.

He handed me a black scarf. Put this over your eyes, and lay down in the back seat. No matter what happens, don't get up or say a word. I could feel the car swirling in and out of traffic, being yelled at and the horns constantly honking. It seemed like hours, and finally the car stopped. I heard nothing. We must have stayed there for 30 minutes. All of a sudden I head the back door open and someone pulling me up.

"What the hell do you think you were doing?" It was Vern, and he was really mad. I took the blind fold off and saw his face red as a beet, his eyes almost popping out of his head. "I thought you sent the taxi" I said meekly. He lit into me with no mercy. Did he give you a password? Did he mention my name? I wouldn't have even bother to come in looking for you but someone saw your name on the TWA manifest. I told him I though he had arranged the ticket. He knew nothing about it. "Well, that means there on to us, so you're going out the back door. I hope you got everything you need to the hotel room, we'll mail it to you later. This is it for you kid. I'll probably never see you again. You need to set your priorities in life. You have so much to offer, find something in life that will fulfill this wanderlust you have. Abdullah will take you the rest of the way. What ever you do don't speak. You will be his subservient wife, all wrapped up in a black package. Have a wonderful, fruitful life. Now, get out of my life!" He turned and started walking away. I just stood there staring at him. Then he stopped and turned around again, motioning me to come to him. I went and stood in front of him, expecting him to give me the riot act again. He put his hand under my chin and turned my face up-wards. "I've always wondered what it would be like if we'd met at a different time in our lives, different circumstances. Do you believe in sole mates? I feel we need more time together, but I don't think it's going to be in this lifetime. You have touched my heart, when I've been trained to have no feelings. I wish we could have our lives setting in front of a fireplace, making love, or running through the ocean together. Next lifetime!" Then he started kissing my eyes, my cheeks, and put his lips very so softly on mine. I could feel his tongue going over my lips, then into my mouth. He squeezed me so tight I could hardly breath. He let go of me gently, pulling his hand from my back and running them over my breast. He turned sharply, and ran away this time.

Abdullah was gently nudging my arm. We must leave immediately. I was given a black galabeyya with the headpiece covering everything but a small slit for my eyes. It was of fine silk. I was told my name was Mona, and I was the wife of a wealthy Saudi. I was not to speak a word, and keep my head down at all times. They gave me brown contact lends for my eyes, and a black wig. Abdullah changed into a silk Saudi costume, with the red and white headscarf. We switched into a silver Mercedes with a driver. I sat in back by myself and he sat up front with the driver.

I seemed like we went for hours, and then we were at a checkpoint. I think it was Port Said. They didn't even bother checking me, as I would have been on my husbands passport, like a peace of property. I heard the guard ask if I wanted to use the facilities, he knew it had been a long drive. I heard him say la la shukran, meaning no thank you. I know I wasn't suppose to say anything but I really had to go to the bathroom. It was as if this had taken over my whole life, I suppose this could be used as a form of torture, not letting someone go to the bathroom. Abdullah must have been a mind reader, as he said softly to me. "In about ten minutes we will be where there are clean restroom facilities on a boat. Don't accept the one's on land, do not leave my side."

Then I felt the car stop abruptly, and Abdullah starting to talk harshly to me. We must be where there are other people around. Keep my head down and my legs crossed! "Yella, yella, yella" he was yelling. Hurry up. I kept my head down and scurried after Abdullah. Vendors were trying to stop me and sell their wares. He yelled at them to leave me alone, and gave them baksheesh. We started going up some stairs. When I glanced up we were boarding a hugh yacht. It must have been 200 feet long. Yella, yella, yella, Abdullah yelled at me. We kept going down corridors, up another flight of stairs, and turning. Finally he opened a door. "Lock the door and don't answer it for anyone except Vern's code." He slammed the door and I heard his footsteps down the corridor. I didn't know what Vern's code was! No one had told me! First priorities go to the bathroom. It felt so good to empty my bladder, I never even noticed that the bathroom fixtures were made of gold till I went to wash my hands. The room was actually as large as my house was on Kauai. You could tell everything was very expensive. I even think I recognized an original oil painting.

I don't wish to speak of my trip off the yacht, as it might be a regular S.O.S. route. I landed on Oahu with no one expecting me, not knowing where I was going to go. I found out later the Wednesday TWA flight that I was supposes to be on had been sabotaged. Someone had planted a small explosive in the window and a woman and he child was sucked out the window. You guessed it, the seat number was the one I had been assigned!

THE FINAL COMMANDMENTS

A new semester was beginning at the University. Perhaps I would just update some classes and stay at University housing. This would solve my problems of housing and a car, and give me time to think.

It seemed strange to be where everything worked. In Egypt the phones very seldom worked. Once they changed everyone's phone number, but they didn't bother to tell you what your new number was. When someone called and it was the wrong number, you would beg them to tell you what number they dialed, so you would know your new number!

I had been gone six years, and the Internet had evolved with people being able to go online and search information. There were several companies, like BRS and Dialog that would let you search for a fee. The problem was, no one knew how to search. It would take them hours, which they were paying for by the minute, to find anything. This gave opportunities to qualified people to fill this need. It was so interesting to think that you could call up some organization and get up to date information. Would this eventually make libraries obsolete?

I kept remembering the things Monk Arsenios was teaching me. I wanted to find some books on these subjects. I'd asked about a metaphysical bookstore and someone had said there was a good one at Unity Church at Diamond Head. I didn't want to get mixed up with any church, but I figured I could just go in the bookstore and leave. The bookstore smelled so good, and the chimes and colors were so relaxing. All of a sudden I heard this beautiful music. I asked, "Is that the tape of the Cazimero Brothers?" The laughed and told me that was the Cazimero's, but not a tape. They were the featured entertainers for this Sunday. "But I thought your service was 7 A.M. and 9 A.M.?" I asked puzzled. I had checked earlier in the paper, as I didn't want to have to go to church. "Yes, but we had to add another service there were so many people. So now we have three services. Each week we feature an entertainer from Waikiki. The music was so sweet, I just had to go in and listen to it. I found myself setting down and listening to the sermon. He wasn't preaching at you like they usually do, but mentioning different things you could do on your path. Where you were now was perfect, you were perfect. Life is just a lesson, and you're doing the best you can. I don't think I've ever been to a service where they didn't mention going to hell if you didn't do certain things. Then the beautiful music started again. It resonated with every fiber of my body. It was closing time, what were they doing, someone was reaching for my hand. What is this? Then we all started singing, "Let there be peace on earth, and let it begin with me." When I finished the song, I was crying. I thought of all the turmoil in the world, people fighting over religion, beliefs, and land. Here I was in this beautiful spot, with all these wonderful plants, a cool breeze and beautiful music. Everyone should be experiencing this. Why aren't they?

As you go out everyone is laughing, and very friendly. I went back to the bookstore and was asking about books on certain topics. This book would cover your interest, she replied. In fact we're starting a class on it this week if you'd be interested.

What is that word, serepentity? But Monk Arsenios said there are no accidents, the universe brings what you need together at the proper time. The Universal law of divine order, natural balance, not accidents. I signed up for the class. My evenings were free. I noticed a sign for a helper in the bookstore. I told the clerk I was a librarian and might be interested in part time work. Since the class started on Tuesday, I told her I'd bring a resume by. Why don't you take a moment now and speak with the Associate Minister, she's here now, and won't be Tuesday evening. I agreed, and kept browsing in the bookstore while she made a phone call.

Have you ever met someone and it's like you've known each other all your life? That was what this meeting was like. We introduced ourselves, and I explained my situation and the hours of my classes. She was fascinated with the online searching I was learning. Abruptly she said, "When can you start?" I told her as long as we could work around my classes, anytime. She told me to come in tomorrow at 8 A.M. "But I thought the bookstore didn't open on Mondays?" I replied. Then she laughed. Forget about that, she said, I need an Assistant, someone that can take instructions and get things done. You're it!

That's how I got started on my spiritual journey. I just needed the right avenue, and this was it. Different strokes for different folks. They had classes which I attended in the evening. The State of Hawaii uses really unique ways of keeping outsiders from getting jobs. One of them in the State Library System is you have to sign up on a list before you can apply for a position. Of course this list is only open certain times, which makes it harder for outsiders. I just automatically put my name on the list at the University.

One day I received a call from the Head Librarian on Kauai. They had a position open, would I want to come for an interview. I really hadn't thought about working in a regular library. I wouldn't be able to make the dates they had open for the interview. They would extend the dates. I couldn't make the hours they had as I worked and went to school. They would do it on the weekend. I felt embarrassed giving so many excuses, so I agreed to an interview. I hadn't been back to see my old friends. I'd go for a visit. The interview was short, and they hired me right away. I told them I had commitments and couldn't get there for a month. That's fine, the library was in renovation, they would wait. What could I say? Was this one of the pathways Monk Arsenios was talking about? I certainly didn't see where I would be learning spiritual things there, it wasn't like where I was now. The semester was almost finished, and I had to make some decision. Perhaps the decision was being made for me.

It appeared that I was going backwards, not forward. I had friends from bridge that I stayed with till I found a place. I was to take training at a temporary small building they were using, then be transferred to another library until ours reopened after renovation. I was always joking with this one person and telling him to behave or I'd turn my Kahuna on him. He mentioned they were having a course on Shaman and Kahuna training, why don't I just take that and cut out the middleman. I looked at the paper. The class would be staring next week. What was one of the last things Ray Hee said to me? You should learn the ways of the Kahuna. I spoke with my supervisor and asked if I could take leave, since the library wasn't open, for the class.

No one could believe that I could actually just start work and take leave. It had never been done before. But they seemed to want me more than I wanted them. This turned out to be more than coincidence. The Shaman had actually lived in Africa, and I had read one of his books on Pyramid Power. I was beginning to see the patterns that Monk Arsenios was always talking about.

10

SHAMAN KAHUNA TRAINING

While preparing for my workshop, I kept thinking of Monk Arsenios telling me to watch for the connections, and Ray Hee reminding me to take some training from a Kahuna. The workshop was held in a remote, plush area of the island, right on the ocean.

Twenty of us from all over the world showed up. I was surprised to find people from Denmark, Germany, and even New Zealand. These people obviously had money, and it surprised me to find CEO's out in the middle of nowhere looking for their essence or spirit! When I started really analyzing the situation, I wondered what I was looking for. Since leaving Egypt my life had been in turmoil. I felt no peace. I wondered constantly, "Where do I belong? What am I supposed to do with the rest of my life?"

LUTISHA TESAREK

The Shaman, Keoki Maki, started the introduction. "You are here for a reason, and probably not the one you thought you were coming for. Some of you think you are here for health, relationships, power, or just to discover where you fit into this great universe. I tell you this, you will be forming a new support group that will be instrumental in helping heal the universe. The more people understand these powers, and use them for the upward movement of mankind, the sooner the world will have peace. Unfortunately, religions have been aware of this energy for centuries, and have kept it hidden so people have to go to the church for their needs. Now governments have discovered this power and are using it to control the people."

That left me wondering more than ever.

The housing was a YMCA camp with community bunks. I got the feeling some of these people had never had to share space before. This must be part of their lesson. The restrooms and showers were across the field without too much privacy. Some of the women came in with silk makeup bags smelling like they had just walked out of a Ralph Lauren salon. They put on their silk nighties and tried to keep their $300 shoes from getting mud on them.

The workshop was more like boot camp. Before the week was up, they would be wearing flip flops and t-shirts to bed. I didn't think any of our lives would ever be the same.

I have taken hundreds of workshops and always bonded with the participants. From my studies, I learned that everyone who crosses your path is there for a reason. You're either leaning a lesson, or giving one. This workshop would be the embodiment of the Universal Law of fellowship: where two or more people of the same vibrations are gathered together, the combined energy towards their purpose is doubled, or even tripled.

I became especially fond of a Professor of Physics from M.I.T. He had been dragged to the conference under false pretenses; he thought he was going on a vacation in the wilderness. He didn't particularly like being around people. He didn't feel comfortable with the social graces; his books and research were his life. He didn't come to the first two sessions, but spent time on the beach and collecting shells. Apparently something the Shaman was saying attracted him at this session, as he came into the circle and sat down.

We had just finished listening to one of the Shaman's parables. "How would you like to have a companion or assistant that accepted whatever you said, did whatever you asked, didn't change anything you thought, filed everything in perfect order and returned it to you exactly as you gave it to them? Even your thoughts would be categorized and filed. The assistant wouldn't think, argue, judge, analyze, question or make decisions, but accepted impressions easily."

I let out one of my extremely loud laughs and bellowed, "I'll take two please" and the group answered, "Make it three!"

"But you all already have this," the leader said quietly, "it is your subconscious."

Perhaps it was his statement, in his usual deep, forceful voice, that attracted the Professor.

What if I told you half of what you believed was not true? I'm sure in your University studies you had to study mythology and folklore. Some of you, especially the ones going into pure research and the scientific fields, probably thought it to be a wasted course. Believe me when I tell you these were probably some of most important classes you took. The courses helped you to recognize certain things as just myths, oral literature, superstitions, and legends. So they were filed in your subconscious as just that, stories and untruths. Yet we store mythologies all though our lives as truth, because of the people that give us the information.

This brings us to our first Kahuna statement: IKE: The world is what you think it is.

This sounded vaguely familiar to me. I checked my notes from Monk Arsenios for the Universal Laws. Ah, there it was -- the Law of Self Truth, truth is what works for you.

We were into the lesson. Everyone started getting their notebooks ready to write down information.

"It starts with our parents."

I felt the Professor start to get up to leave, so I reached over and took his arm. He yanked his arm away and gave me a dirty look.

I just smiled and pushed a note to him that read, "This subject won't last long, the good stuff comes in a few minutes." He was on his knees ready to bolt from the circle, but finally sat back down.

Shaman Maki continued. "I noticed from the enrollment forms that two of you are psychiatrists. You can thank all the parents for your lucrative professions. We are born as perfect little human beings. Then we start listening to adults around us who pass on their fears, failures, and start criticizing us and limiting our dreams. Louise Hay has an excellent book called You Can Heal Your Life. She even goes so far as to suggest we choose our own parents to learn our lessons in this life."

"Hmmm," I thought, "that fits another Universal Law. Magnetic Affinities: you choose your astrological time and date of birth, lessons to be learned, parents, strengths and weakness."

His statement unleashed feelings in everyone! I could see denial, pain, anger, and sadness in some of the participants' faces. I was surprised that the Professor showed no emotion at all. I thought he would try to leave again after that statement. After a very heated debate, the shaman ended the outburst. "That is Louise Hay's belief, you don't have to believe it!"

He went on. "This next statement will probably offend the doctors in the conference. Louise also lists 62 pages of medical problems, what thoughts have created them, and the affirmation to correct your thought pattern. What are the biggest causes of health problems? Thoughts of fear, anger, guilt, and unforgiveness. Many of these are mentioned in the Bible."

I was surprised that didn't cause a big reaction like his other statement. It did bring up a question from one of the physicians. "So in summation you are trying to put all of us out of business?'" There was a big laugh.

"On the contrary, I'm trying to make your work easier. Once you accept these energy patterns, you will know where to look for the problems.

This brings us to our second Kahuna statement: Makia: Energy flows where attention goes.

"Yes," I rememberd, "that's the same as the Universal Law of Attraction."

The shaman was explaining. "Everything is energy, which means thought is energy and can be converted into another kind of energy. When groups of people are in a room and do breathing or meditative exercises, energy is created. Literally your thoughts, with emotion and belief, manifest physical situations. This will be our exercise for tonight. Remember that the exercise is to help you heal your problems, it's not for me. The person sitting to your left will be your partner. I know some of you don't like speaking with strangers. But I guarantee you, before this week is up, there will be no strangers in this group, and you will know your root problem. Whether or not you want to do something about it is up to you. If you don't feel comfortable talking with someone else, just sit in the silence together. Believe me, the person to your left is not there by accident. The two of you have something to say that will help the other."

I blushed at this, because I really forced the Professor to stay in the group. This was going to be really uncomfortable.

I looked at him and laughed. He didn't laugh or say anything. We just started walking away from the group. He then said with a sigh, "You didn't drag me, I came back on my own. This is why I came back."

I looked at him with surprise. "You came back to do an exercise?" Then he finally smiled and laughed. "No, I came back to see why you're always laughing. Why are you so happy?"

This came as real surprise to me. I had never really thought of myself as really happy, especially now in this transition period of my life. I felt like I was in transit limbo, waiting for my next stop. "I never realized that people think of me as really happy. So perhaps I'm misjudging when I ask why are you so unhappy?"

He looked me square in the eye with no emotion and I thought he was just going to turn and go ask for another partner. We just stood there for about two minutes staring each other down.

Finally he said, "Fair question. I guess you've already figured I don't like to be around groups of people. Let's go for a swim."

I decided to let him make the rules and followed him to the beach. He dropped his books on the beach, took off his shirt and thongs, and ran into the water. I know he was waiting for me to complain about being too cold, or not having a bathing suit, so I just jumped in with my clothes on. When I finally caught up with him I saw pure delight on his face. He was now in his element, with nature and in control. I had the feeling this was the happiest he'd been in a long time.

Suddenly, he got serious again. "Okay, here are the rules. You don't ask me any personal questions, I just volunteer what I want to talk about. You can say anything you want, I'll listen. Everything said and discussed here between us does not leave the camp; it's what the attorneys among us would call privileged information."

All of a sudden he disappeared and I saw air bubbles coming up. When he surfaced he said with no expression in his voice, "Give me your clothes." I just looked at him, and could tell this was not a sexual request, I doubt if that word was even in his vocabulary. I took it as a test, and took off my shorts and shirt and gave them to him. He disappeared below the water, taking my clothes to secure under a rock. "I caught a glimpse of his bare white bottom as he went down. When he came back up, he actually smiled. "Now we are in our original state, naked and innocent. This is the first time I've been skinny-dipping. They will never believe me when I return to the University."

His next statement surprised me. "I guess since we're naked together I should know your name." I could see he thought he'd made a really big joke. "You can call me Brad."

"My name is Natasha." I answered. We started our dialogue treading water.

"How important do you think a name is?" he asked me. " Is a rose a rose by any other name?"

I told him in my studies a name was supposedly important for the number of letters for numerology, and in some cultures one's name changed at difference stages in life. Women had to take on their husband's name, thus losing part of their own identity.

"If you had told me your name was Carl," I added, 'you would still be the same person to me. A name only identifies the ethnic group a person belongs to."

He seemed satisfied with my answer. He let out a wonderful laugh, and started swimming out towards the ocean. I followed him until I was too tired to go on. I just floated on my back, trying to get my breath. I looked up at the sky and wondered at all the beautiful stars, and pondered a parallel universe. I shut my eyes and listened to the sound of the ocean.

What a wonderful peaceful time. I was remembering all the times I had skinny-dipped. In high school my girlfriend and I climbed over the municipal pool fence after midnight. It felt so good to be free, and there was the thrill of the danger that you would be caught. In the Turks & Caicos Islands we used to go in the evenings with the children. I thought about swimming at a pool in a private home when I visited my daughter while at the University, and now this time. Each time held a different feeling because of the people I was with and the place. Floating peacefully, I decided I could get used to this. I heard a splash and put my feet in the water. Brad was returning.

"I suppose you do this all the time. I understand there's a beach for nude sunbathing on Kauai?"

I answered "Yes, that's true, Donkey Beach. But I've never been there. Why would you think I do this all the time?"

He just couldn't believe a person would live where it was possible and not take advantage of it. I replied if a person had a good paying position, like a Professor, then he could afford to go on vacations where he could do these things.

"That is true," he answered, "but you have to be adventurous to go to new places. I just have never cared to go out of my comfort zone.

"Then why are you here?" I asked him. He reminded me of our agreement of no personal questions.

I started swimming back to the beach. "Hey, don't you want your clothes?" he yelled.

I was hoping no one was on the beach listening to us. I sat down in the shallow water and waited for him to bring me my clothes. The smile on his face told me he knew he was in control. Why was it so important for him to always be in control? Why did I care? At workshops like these, there would be a different partner or group for each activity.

The shaman had said I was supposed to get some lesson out of this experience, but I sure couldn't figure out what it was. I decided maybe I was giving the lesson instead of getting it.

We dried off on the beach, and he asked if I was hungry. I told him I was, but not enough to drive twenty miles to get something to eat. The kitchen had been locked for over five hours.

"Ah, but I have a key," he said as he smiled sheepishly.

I started to question him, but he just replied, "Don't ask."

We went into the kitchen but didn't turn on any lights, which led me to believe the key was not legal. We fixed a sandwich, took some chips and a drink, and left. He motioned me to follow him. Apparently, during the two days he hadn't been to classes he'd checked the whole area out. He took us to a lovely location hidden in a cove. We spread out a towel and had our picnic. We didn't talk but seemed to just enjoy each other's company. Maybe he was just a loner who didn't have any social graces.

I have always been one to draw people out and make them feel comfortable. I've moved around so much, I know what it's like to be an outsider who is ignored by everyone. Then again, he could have had a bad relationship and didn't want to be around another human being. Some people gave up after one try at life.

A sudden Hawaiian downpour developed. He gathered up everything and ran under a tree. Actually he had stashed some things under there; blankets, radio, and even reading material.

"We would never make it back in this downpour, so let's sit it out here," he suggested. "We'll change the rules. We may each ask one question, but we have the right to refuse to answer."

I was trying to think of something to ask that he would answer. I knew he wouldn't answer anything personal, so I thought maybe a question about work might be safe. I thought the Pyramids would be safe.

"I lived in Egypt," I began, "and it amazes me how many people still believe the men who dragged those huge stones and built the Pyramids to mathematical formulas did not know they were building them to mathematical formulas."

THE FINAL COMMANDMENTS

He had a big smile on his face. He was happy with the subject.

"If I believed any of this stuff the Kahuna is teaching, then I would know we were put together for this purpose. I have spent twenty years of research on this theory. You can't get anyone to fund this type research, unless it can be used to build some sort of war machine, so I have been doing it on my own. I know you're probably going to think I'm ready for the nut house, but half of my theory has been proven.

"I'm sure a laser beam and levitation were used to build the Pyramids. Already IBM has invented a microchip that floats in the air. All you have to do is expand that energy field and you will have levitation. That could explain how the large blocks for the Pyramid were moved and fitted into perfect alignment.

Some of my original research included work by a tenth century Arab historian, known as the Herodotus of the Arabs. He talked about a "magic papyrus" being placed under the stones to be moved. Then the stone was struck with a metal rod that caused the stone to levitate and move along a path paved with stones and fenced on either side by metal poles. In following his theory, if you can detect the position of an object in space and feed it into a control system which can vary the strength of electromagnets which are acting on the object, it is not difficult to keep it levitated. You just have to program the system to weaken the strength of the magnet whenever the object approaches it and strengthen when it moves away. You could even do it with movable permanent magnets. These methods violate the assumption that the magnets are fixed. Electromagnetic suspension is one system used in magnetic levitation trains referred to as maglev, such as the one at Birmingham airport, England.

It has become common place to see the new high temperature superconducting materials levitated in this way. A superconductor is perfectly diamagnetic which means it expels a magnetic field. Other diamagnetic materials are common place and can also be levitated in a magnetic field if it is strong enough. In diamagnetics, electrons adjust their trajectories to compensate the influence of the external magnetic field and this results in an induced magnetic field which is directed in the opposite direction. It means that the induced magnetic moment is anti-parallel to the external field. Superconductors are diamagnetics with the macroscopic change in trajectories, screening current at the surface."

"Can you please explain that to me in simple terms?" I asked.

"As you might well know, all matter in the universe consists of small particles called atoms and each atom contains electrons that circle around a nucleus. This is how the world is made. If one places an atom, or a large piece of a matter containing billions and billions of atoms, in a magnetic field, electrons doing their circles inside do not like this very much. They alter their motion in such a way as to oppose this external influence. This is the most general principle of nature. Whenever one tries to change something settled and quiet, the reaction is always negative. So, according to this principle, the disturbed electrons create their own magnetic field and as a result the atoms behave as little magnetic needles pointing in the direction opposite to the applied field."

My mouth fell open, this had been my theory all along. He saw my expression and thought I was mocking him.

"What, you think this is too unbelievable?"

THE FINAL COMMANDMENTS

"No, no" I answered. "This has been my theory all along. I know the Pyramid is not a burial chamber. It's five square blocks of stone, with only two small rooms about less than 50 feet by 35 feet. There aren't any hieroglyphics on the walls. The measurements are the same as many mathematical formulas for time and distance."

He was happy to know someone outside of Physics could believe it to be true. "My question to you will be, why are you here? You can take the question anyway you want. By here I could mean here at this class, living here on Kauai, on here in this universe at this time."

I thought that would be easy to answer, but when I thought about it for a minute, it was a deep, soul-searching question.

"The answer to why I'm at this workshop is I because I was advised by two important people in my life that this would be part of my learning experience. Why I'm on Kauai at this time, I'm not sure. I just moved back and haven't figured that out yet. One of the Universal Laws is Growth doesn't come without discontent, the need for a challenge. Even living in paradise I'm not content or really happy. For some reason this must be a time of learning for me. Why am I in the universe at this time? I believe I'm here to play some small part in a group conscious effort, that's why I'm always going to conferences and workshops. I know from the life I've lived so far, it's not just for my pleasure. I'm to contribute to something, but I haven't found that out yet."

We talked for hours, mostly about his project. Half of it I didn't understand, but in general it did make sense to me. All of a sudden we realized the sun was coming up. We had been talking for over eight hours. I went to the cottage and just hit the bunk and went to sleep. I didn't go to breakfast so I could sleep longer.

That day's lecture started with more information about the Shaman traditions. In Hawaiian it was called Huna, meaning hidden knowledge. As a librarian, I believed that knowledge held secret isn't helping anyone. It's like having a wonderful library with all the knowledge of the world, but the door is locked. The Shaman training consisted of chants, which are recognized as affirmations, and breathing exercises.

Shaman began. "The subconscious mind doesn't distinguish between past, present, and future, the present is all there is. Your present circumstances are the effect of thoughts, decisions and actions in the past. You've probably heard of this referred to as Karma, or cause and effect, which brings us to Manawa; Now is the moment of power. Now would be defined as the range of present attention. Most people live in the past, always second guessing what they should have done or said. It's a waste of energy. Your assignment for tonight is to become aware of the present moment."

At lunch, we ended up sitting next to the big shot lawyer from New York that was disruptive and always negative in the class. Nothing he had said would give any insight to what was bothering him. Another person at the table made the comment that if we were on a higher spiritual level there would be no need for lawyers. That did it! The lawyer was so mad I thought he was going to jump over the table and take the man on.

"Oh yeah?" he yelled. "Well, if we didn't have any lawyers, who would protect you against big blood sucking companies that overcharge us and have no safety standards?"

The other gentleman replied, "That's what our government is supposed to do."

The lawyer argued, "Yes, you said that right, is SUPPOSED to do! Where was our government on September 11?"

Everything went quiet. The man said apologetically, "No one could have seen that coming and prevented it!"

The lawyer was infuriated now! "Don't give me that bull! I've been researching this for over two years because my wife was in that building! I know many people in high places in our government that are telling the real truth. Of course the United States government knew about September 11 before it happened. Why do you think they rushed to the unprecedented legal process of paying off the families of the people killed in the World Trade Center? The government was warned by the intelligence agencies of Israel, Egypt, U.K., Germany, and the Philippines. Not just once, but several times. Their ego was so pumped up with our destructive war machine their imagination couldn't conceive of such a thing, even though for years they had been saying that was what they were going to do.

The intelligence agencies had picked up on a plot by Muslim terrorists to hijack jetliners and crash them into US landmarks. Through questioning an Iranian man the officials were informed of an attack that was to take place the week of September 10. If the government took this seriously, why would the President be off reading to schoolchildren as far away as he could get? I'd like to see the job description for the President that states the priorities of his position, which some have called the most powerful person in the world. Is reading books to school children at the top of the list? How much did that reading cost, when you figure in the cost of Air Force One, the Secret Service, etc?

Even a retired FBI counter terrorism chief stated they had indications this was coming for years. On evacuation at the Capitol building Congressman Ike Skelton, a member of the Armed Services Committee, said the CIA warned that there could be an attack – AN IMMINENT ATTACK - of this nature, so this is not entirely unexpected. A congressman told us it was not unexpected! Where was our government?

So what happens to the government people who are sworn to protect us in the country with the greatest intelligence system in the world? The head of the agency who knew beforehand about this and did nothing gets the highest medal for service, while the Congressmen who vote on these matters and sit on the committees have cut their work time in half, down to only a hundred days a year! They justify tacking provisions on to a bill that has the name Patriot or Child in the title, that allows recruiters on campuses and forces the schools to give lists of the students, or taking away our civil liberties, because they don't have enough time to pass all the bills. Of course they don't have enough time. They only work one third of the year. This is the same Congress that didn't have time to extend unemployment benefits before taking a vacation break, but had time to vote themselves a raise. What company do you know who gives you a lifetime retirement of $15,000 per month after a couple of years of service? None, because they would go bankrupt, which is what is happening to America. Congress doesn't have to pay a penny towards this retirement. A military person stays in twenty years, and maybe he'll get $1,000 a month retirement. Now you tell me whom the Congress is making the laws for!

He was on a roll now.

THE FINAL COMMANDMENTS

The government needs to change its emblem from an Eagle to a condom because that more accurately reflects the government's political stance. It allows for inflation, halts production, destroys the next generation, protects a bunch of pricks, and gives you a sense of security while you're actually being screwed."

Everyone took a little breather with that and laughed.

"So," someone ventured, "you don't think the people in the World Trade Center should have received any compensation?"

"No, I didn't say that. I'm saying, 'look at the reason for it.' You know, many families saw the settlement as a cover-up for the government's blunder. They refused the money and demanded an investigation. I'm part of that group that wanted the investigation.

People who took the money had to sign a document stating they wouldn't sue anyone. A sheik from Saudi Arabia offered one million dollars to a fund for the 9/11 victims, and it was refused as they felt the Saudi's were in someway responsible. This is why the victim's families didn't want to accept the money. Thank heaven for their courage, otherwise we wouldn't have had the 9/11 report.

This has set a precedent. Now the Oklahoma City bombing relatives want some compensation. If you want to look at it from a fairness point of view, a solder killed in action gets $6,000. Why is his blood less precious than someone in the World Trade Center? In truth, he has also been put in harm's way because the government isn't doing its job.

If the government would let the State Department do their job, which is to have dialogue and handle international matters, you wouldn't be having these senseless undeclared wars. Instead, the Executive Branch sets the goals that include the great war machine with such benefactors as the Carlyle Foundation, Arbusto, and Halliburton to mention a few. I call it fictitious reasons for fictitious wars.

I would love to see the holdings of all the politicians in companies involved in materials for the support of wars. It wouldn't do any good to make the list of names public, as the lawyers are the ones that make the rules for blind trusts and places to hide stock. Of course, the President puts his stock in a 'blind trust' with no knowledge of what they do with it. Now, if you were the manager for the President, would you invest in Johnson & Johnson baby wipes or Halliburton?"

The other man suggested, "I guess you feel we should have just let them come on over and take over our country, just wait till Iraq was ready to drop a bomb?"

The reply was fast and sharp.

"Don't tell me you're still dragging that old bone around. Even your spin-doctors can't sell that again. The worst part about that is they took a thousand of our most qualified men and had them spend years looking for weapons of mass destruction, in order to justify the war. To me, that was the worst abuse of our military personnel on the front lines. They were sent in harm's way without even understanding what the Iraqis were tying to tell them. We invade a country and don't even have the courtesy to have someone that speaks their language. How many American and Iraqis lives could have been saved if there were American military personnel who were fluent enough in the native language to prevent any misunderstanding in what was being said? Besides that, the men were sitting on the border for months with no one in charge who would spend the time to have them learn the language.

All the government understands is we have big bombs, we have the tanks, and we have the planes, so bring it on! So there's collateral damage, even if it's our own Americans on the front line, our collocation of the willing, or some Iraqis. That's part of the game plan.

You wouldn't try to sell the idea that this undeclared war plan just started after 9/11 because there's just too much documentation available for contradiction. America's corporate merchants of death were at it as early as 1983. Mr. Rumsfeld, as a private citizen, was over shaking hands with Saddam and arranging an oil pipeline joint venture, sponsored through the Agriculture Department with guaranteed loans worth millions. This was during the first Bush Presidency. Guess what? Iraq defaulted on the loans, and guess who paid for it? You, the good old tax payer.

There was a detailed invasion plan for Iraq years ago. The invading army detailed the division of assets of Iraq, even selling off some oil fields. It was in such detail, they had even rewritten Iraq's copyright laws. The Corporate takeover was in place; all they needed was an excuse for an invasion.

Why would the government insiders get excited about a little old attack on America? After all, the first World Trade Center attack involved just a few floors, and it was repaired. A big attack would unite the country; we could send our spin doctors out with innuendoes and half truths connecting it to Iraq. We could pass a law for our safety giving the bigshots all the power they need. When people are living in fear, they give away all their power to the government.

"The corporate bigshots may have had to wait twenty years, but they'll get their own personal oil fields in the Middle East."

Furious, the man's opponent lashed back. "Talk about talking out of both sides of your mouth! You claim President Bush isn't very smart, and in the next breath you say he's planned to rule the Middle East."

Laughing robustly, which really irritated the other man, he replied, "No, a small group of neocon defense intellectuals headed by Wolfowitz took advantage of Bush's ignorance and inexperience. Being raised in west Texas, he absorbed the Texan cultural combination of machismo, anti-intellectualism and overt religious zeal. But as President Truman said, 'The buck stops here.' It is his responsibility to investigate what he is told."

The second man was horrified that an American could talk like this. He wanted to get him in a corner. "You are not a true patriot. Certainly you can't believe what you just said?"

He was fast and furious with his reply. "If you refuse to look at history and the facts, then you are the one who is not a patriot! America is supposed to be for Americans, not the politicians and corporate mongers that prey on every loophole in the laws to make a buck off the American taxpayer. Ancient Rome collapsed because the empire grew too complex and expensive to operate in the face of dangers."

I immediately recalled an article by John Wong I had read in the Wichita Eagle. It about summed up the process. Wong wrote, "A democracy cannot exist as a permanent form of government. It can only exist until the voters discover that they can vote themselves money from the Public Treasury. From that moment on the majority always votes for the candidates promising the most benefits from the public Treasury with a result that a democracy always collapses over loose fiscal policy followed by dictatorship. The average age of the world's greatest civilizations has been 200 years."

I suddenly realized the man spoke some truth. I thought, "Everybody has to lobby now. Kansas, as a state, had to spend one million dollars lobbying to keep their military bases off the list to be cut. If the Federal Government worked on merit and need, the State could be spending that money on the people of Kansas. But they know how the system works. Are we, as Americans," I wondered, "going to break this mold, or follow in history?"

My mind was spinning as the lawyer continued spouting.

"Already the government is going to extremes to sell their great lie about defending America. They are still spending billions on military equipment that's outdated and not relevant to the way military actions will be fought in the future. There is no fear of our military might. Didn't Vietnam teach us anything? They are ruining the fiber of the American family. Having undeclared wars releases the government from the requirement to sell war to Congress. Since the 1975 draft was eliminated, the military is dominated by the educationally and economically disadvantaged, the underachievers who desperately need a job and the money. They set unrealistic goals, giving recruiters access to schools without permission. If they refuse, then they can take away funding. The recruiters under unrealistic numbers make fake school certificates and reports on the use of drugs. They even disrupt the lives of our National Guard, who signed up to defend problems in the United States, not on foreign soil.

Maybe Dwight D. Eisenhower said it best. 'Every gun that is made, every warship launched, every rocket fired, signifies in the final sense a theft from those who hunger and are not fed, those who are cold and not clothed."

Right now the United States is loathed by most foreign populations and nearly all governments. The Mayor of Newfoundland, whose city graciously took care of all the people that landed there instead of the United States on 9-11, made the statement no one would do this to us, because no one hates us. The government is using fear to manipulate the public."

I think everyone was relieved when lunch was over. This had not been a peaceful lunch, but the lawyer did bring up some good points. Were we, ARE we just going to sit back and believe everything the government tells us?

The Shaman started off with a meditation. When we were all centered, he brought up the heated discussion at lunch.

"I've been asked how can we stay centered and forgive when these terrible things are happening to us? I think I will take a few minutes to try and explain something. Whatever is happening to us now, as a nation or individual, has been manifested from our own thoughts and actions."

I recognized in that statement the Universal Law Magnetic Affinity: you determine the effects on your life.

The Shaman suggested, "Let's go back to the beginning to see if we can understand our own control.

Many of you are probably familiar of the name Atlantis, which was a prehistoric civilization, which parallels Plato's account in many respects, such as the achievement of a higher civilization. Around 10,500 BC, the Atlanteans created three repositories for the records of their culture and the history of humanity. They were deposited in a "hall of records" in Egypt, Tibet, and South America. This was so if there were a shift in the earth at least one would survive. Because of the misapplication of power, Atlantis was going to be destroyed. It appears this is where our world is again. When the soul evolution of humanity reaches the point where individuals' experience is in accord with the divine, rather than using the power for selfish motives, the depositories and secret information will be revealed.

Egypt was actually the chosen land before Israel, but the Pharoahs started infighting, and the chosen land was moved to Israel.

Perhaps it would help if I explained how we ended up on earth in this body form. Our soul evolution will help you understand some of the myths and also stories in the Bible that have formed your belief systems. The solar system attracted souls, and since each system is a single expression, with its planets as integral parts, the earth came into the path of souls. It was an expression of God with its own laws, its own plan, its own evolution. Souls, longing to feel the beauty of earth and plants, mixed with them and expressed themselves through them. They also mingled with the animals, and made, in imitation of them, thought forms: they played at creating; they imitated God. But it was a playing, an imitating, that interfered with what had already been set in motion, and what had been set in motion gradually entangled the souls, so that they became trapped in the plan of earth's evolution, inside the bodies they had themselves created. This is incomprehensible from what man terms the scientific standpoint, for it involves the law of relativity and laws of atomic structure, which have not yet been discovered.

This period in the earth's history, however, is very well-documented: it was the Age of Fable, when gods and goddesses - the souls, roamed the earth, turning into trees, speaking from rocks, and inhabiting the bodies of creatures which were half animal, half human. Sex already existed in the animal kingdom, but the souls, in their thought forms, were androgynous. Therefore, to experience sex, they created thought forms for companions, isolating the negative force in a new thought form, retaining the positive in them. This objectification is what man calls Lilith, the first woman. This entanglement of souls in what man calls matter was a probability from the beginning, but God did not know it would happen, or when, until the souls, of their own choice, had caused it to happen, the free will we were given. Then a way of escape from the predicament was created. A form was chosen to be a proper vehicle of the soul on earth and the way was paved for souls to enter earth and experience it as a part of their cycle.

The form already existing which most approached the needs of the souls was what man would call one of the anthropoid apes. Souls descended on these bodies, hovering above and about them rather than inhabiting them, and influenced them to move toward a different goal than the simple one they had been pursuing. They came down out of the trees, built fires, made tools, lived in communities, and began to communicate with each other. Swiftly, even as man measures time, they lost their animal look, shed bodily hair, and took on refinements of manner and habit. All this was done by the souls working through the glands, until, at last, there was a new inhabitant of the earth, man. He appeared as a consciousness within an animal. Soon he was that which his pattern demanded of objectification in the earth; he was a little higher than the beasts, a little lower than the angels.

There were males and females in these new, pure races; and both had complete souls. Eve replaced Lilith, and became the complement to Adam, the perfect helpmate, and the ideal companion for the three-fold life of earth: physical, mental, and spiritual. In Eve, the positive pole was suppressed and the negative pole expressed; in Adam the negative pole was suppressed, the positive expressed. Which a soul would become was a matter of choice, unless it was already entangled and unbalanced. Eventually the positive-negative would have to be brought in balance, so there was not, basically, any difference. For souls in balance, it was a device for the duration of the earth cycle. It was not a voluntary assumption of an attitude, not a fall into error.

Man became aware, with the advent of his consciousness, that sex meant more to them than to the animals. To man, it represented the door by which new souls were to enter the earth. It was the only means the trapped souls had of getting out of their unfortunate predicament. It worked not as an integral part of creation, of God's mind, as it did in animals, but separately, at the direction of man's own soul. It was a creative power that could be used for good or evil.

The plan for the earth cycle of souls was a series of incarnations, interlocked by periods of dwelling in other dimensions of consciousness in the system - the planets - until every thought and action of the physical body, with its five senses and conscious mind, was in accord with the plan originally laid out for the soul. This conquest of the physical body could not be attained until there was perfection in the other dimensions of consciousness in the system, for, by the law of relativity, these made up, with earth, the total expression of the sun and its satellites.

The race of man was fostered by a soul, which had already returned to God and had become a companion and co-creator with Him. This is the soul man knows as Christ.

The Christ soul was interested in the plight of its brother souls trapped in earth, it took form itself from time to time to act as a leader to the people who were often bewildered. Souls at first only lightly inhabited bodies; they remembered their identity. Gradually, life after life, they descended into earthiness, into less mentality, less consciousness of the mind force. They remembered themselves in dreams, in stories, in fables.

Thus religion came into being, and the arts of music, numbers, and geometry. These were brought to earth by the incoming souls; gradually their heavenly source was forgotten, as the source of the story of themselves and their God was forgotten.

Finally man was left with a conscious mind definitely separated from his own individuality, which he now called the subconscious mind. He felt the influence of himself, and he was able to reason with this conscious mind. Man built up reasons for believing what he felt to be true, but what he no longer knew by inner knowledge. Philosophy and theology resulted. Finally man began to look around him and discover, in the earth, the secrets of which he carried within himself but could no longer reach with his consciousness. The result was science.

The plan went into action. Downward went man from heavenly knowledge to mystic dreams, to revealed religions, to philosophy and theology, until the bottom was reached and there was no more connection with that which he had left. Then he began to fight his way beck toward it with the tool of reason, and with suffering, patience, and faith. Atlantis sank; civilizations rose and fell. Downward he went to the depths of immersion in the consciousness of earth; backward he slowly began to climb.

The Christ soul helped him. He took on flesh, to teach and lead. He realized that He could not show the way to mankind unless He made a pattern for them. He could not descend into their midst and teach them and expect them to follow; He had to suffer and think and experience earth as they did, and show them how to emerge from it. He showed the way: He became the way: He overcame death and the body, and returned to God, laying down the ego of the will, accepting the crucifixion.

You know the world today has reached the great parting of the ways, when the forces that led us downward are making their last stand against the forces that have turned and begun the march upward: this is the darkest hour, the hour before dawn. Hate, prejudice, ignorance, misunderstanding, fear, violence, stalk the land. The point is, we can no longer avoid doing something about it.

Is there anyone who would like to comment on what we can do now about our concerns with the world situation?"

A very mild mannered man who hadn't spoke once stood up.

"If we are concerned about America and what's happening, it is up to us to do something towards the healing process. When I refer to saving America, I'm not talking about saving it from foreigners who hate us so much they need to make as big a statement as possible, consequently 9/11. I'm talking about the politicians who spend more on getting elected than on education. There's something really wrong with that system of government. Then you have the bible thumping hypocrites who take every opportunity to run down a religion, a way of life, a way of living, and what you read I can't help but think how sad their lives must be that they have to spend all their time dictating someone else's life style. Most of these people define "wrong" as that which is different from them. If they really think they are following Jesus, then they'd better remember Jesus taught only love and forgiveness. Separation from God or the Universal power breeds indifference, false superiority. Unity produces compassion, genuine equality.

Call it what you want. God, Universal energy, intuition, that small voice you hear inside you is your gyro. Take heed of it. The soul understands what the mind cannot conceive. The soul creates, the mind reacts. Go with your feeling. The soul talks to you through your feelings. Feelings are the language of the soul. Every thought has energy that transmits its signal through the universe. Every thought you've ever had goes to this energy; it's stored in the Akashic Records. It's also considered the collective consciousness of the universe.

School systems needs to change to a values-based curriculum, instead of just learning facts. Some schools do have Peaceful Conflict Resolutions classes, but we need to include ethical economics, creative consciousness and mind power, tolerance, and anything dealing with creativity from music to art. Teach logic, critical thinking, problem solving, and creation, using the tools of their own initiation. Let there be an awareness of honesty, responsibility, and fairness.

THE FINAL COMMANDMENTS

Our government laws are based on power, not the common good. One simple example, tobacco. The government gives grants to grow it, knows it's unhealthy, even spends millions on advertisement, but does not write a law banning cigarettes. However, hemp is against the law, and not because of health. This weed is no more addictive or a health risk than cigarettes or alcohol, which are both protected by law. It's because hemp is one of the most useful, longest-lasting materials on earth. It's easy to grow, and would produce fiber for clothes, ropes, medicinal properties, and pulp for paper. It would substitute for one-tenth the cost. There's the catch. Cotton growers, nylon, timber products would go out of business. That is the real reason marijuana is illegal. Our government deliberately misleads the people. Deception is part of government. The old saying is, if you lie big enough and long enough, the lie becomes the truth.

The government cannot legislate morality, cannot mandate equality. Laws are usually there to serve the elitist few who will benefit most from them. What is needed is a growth of conscious, not a growth of government. A government is measured by how well it treats the least among its members. Seek to build, not to destroy. Nothing breeds appropriate behavior faster than exposure to the light of public scrutiny. In the U.S. the top 1 ½% hold more wealth than the bottom 90%.

The technology to produce electric cars, provide affordable health care, or produce solar power is already here. The government will not change anything until we insist on it.

We as individuals must step up in this blame game, as we have let the leaders we elected do it for years and years without protesting or questioning. We must realize we are not victims, but full participants. We must take responsibility for our own thoughts, choices, and emotions. Fear is the name of the game. We've let the government scare us into submission. We must direct ourselves and choose to be peaceful inside. We need holistic politicians.

Our fear thoughts are allowing our government to spend tax dollars by the billions on wars instead of education, roads, and our economy. We can literally think this government out, and visualize people to govern that care for the people.

"We need to turn individual awareness into collective action. Stop giving away our power by allowing others to determine what to believe. Peace is the enemy of the ego. Look upon your mind as a garden to be cultivated and nurtured. Nourish the soil with forgiveness. Every meditation, prayer, thought can be a vote to turn the world around.

What you think is what you'll get. What you fear is what you will draw to you. What you resist, persists. What you choose, you experience. The universe is like a great echo chamber, sooner or later what you send out comes back.

Our old systems and institutions are breaking down; ways of life that we consider secure and enduring are suddenly gone. TV and movies are filled with violence and destruction. Politicians and business people are jailed for illegal activities. Our government knows pleasure can be used to enslave a person as effectively as pain.

Spiritual laws are inescapable and impersonal. What is true for a person is true for a country; the golden rule, cause and effect, what goes around comes around. Atonement is part of these spiritual laws. America has much to answer for. We are spending billions to destroy a country and its people, with hopes

177 •

of getting its oil. For the price of one B-2 Bomber, 1.5 billion dollars, we could have 56,000 teachers!" The man sat down.

The Shaman said, "Thank you Henry, that was very perceptive. Tonight's homework will be to concentrate on your environment; become aware of colors, shapes, sounds, your body, smell, taste, and the clothing you're wearing"-- I pushed a note over to Brad that read 'or not wearing' and we giggled like a couple of school kids. "This type of focus is a skill that has to be developed."

The group broke up and I said to Brad, "You want to go focus with me?" He reminded me we'd better get to the kitchen before it's locked up if we're going to focus our taste buds. We both laughed at this. It was nice to have a partner not wanting to discuss old baggage. This was fun. We loaded up on supplies and headed for our little hideaway.

We made sure no one followed us, and then we went for our skinny dip. I laughed and said to Brad as he put my clothes under the rock, "Now remember, if anyone sees us just tell them we're doing our homework, just getting in touch with all our senses." He swam out into the ocean again, and I floated on my back in a meditative state.

I can understand why men get irritated at women for always wanting to be right beside them, asking them what they are thinking. I've lived by myself over twenty-five years and I really like the idea of not always having to explain yourself or keep someone entertained. I'm alone, but never lonely. I think the problem really stems from someone being insecure.

I could hear Brad approaching, so I put my feet down in the water. Someone might think this is strange being concerned about someone seeing your body when you're skinny dipping, but actually you can't see much in the water.

"Did you do your homework?" I asked Brad. He paused for a moment, then said it was different when you're aware of what you're doing. The water felt different, there were sounds of the waves, the taste of the water, and the way the water feels on the different parts of your body.

We went back to our little cove and started to work on the food. We exaggerated sounds as we ate to indicate how delicious it was. Then he seemed to ponder what he was going to say next.

"If I could just forget the past," he began, "then this workshop would be worth it. Do you have any issues with the past?"

"No way, I learned a long time ago once a moment passes, start working on the future. It's just a lesson in life, and if you're smart, you'll learn the lesson the first time. That's why I can't understand people choosing the same type a personal relationship time after time. I imagine you've known people whose lives just seems to always be in turmoil. I learned my lesson, trying to hang on to the past is unhealthy."

I looked at him and his head was hanging down; too much information maybe? "Well, you asked!" I told him.

"I know, I know. I've just never bothered with a personal life and wondered if I missed out on anything. When I retire, what will I do then?"

It amazed me how someone can have no problem at all and then create one. Here's a perfectly healthy man, with a good education, probably no financial concerns, and he's contemplating if the grass was greener on the other side.

THE FINAL COMMANDMENTS

"According to a Monk I spent some time with in a Monastery, we each have a purpose in our lifetime for the planet, so you'll just have to figure out what that is. Then you can dedicate your retirement time to fulfilling your destiny."

We both looked at each other and started laughing. "Right" he replied. "Like I'm so special I can change the world and make it a better place."

Again we talked until almost sunrise. This was the first time I had spent this much time with a man without any sort of physical relationship. Perhaps one of my lessons is the way I use relationships in my life, or let them use me. It felt good to be on an intellectual level with someone instead of physical.

Our last class was where the shaman promised us the answer to everything. We started with a meditation and visualization technique. I was so tired I drifted of to la la land. Brad poked me when he saw me starting to tip over.

"Better wake up," Brad whispered. "He's going to give us the final piece of puzzle to the jigsaw of life.

In his deep voice, the Shaman started, "The final philosophy is Mana: All power comes from within. Another Universal Law of Abundance, you have everything you need inside you. Huna philosophy teaches that the power that creates your experience comes from your own body, mind, and spirit. Nothing ever happens to you without your participation. You attract it through your beliefs, desires, fears, and expectations. I leave you with this simply technique that is the simplest way to create your desires. BLESS EVERYONE AND EVERYTHING THAT REPRESENTS WHAT YOU WANT. You can do this several ways. One is admiration, giving compliment or praise;

affirmations, a statement of blessing for what you desire; and appreciation, giving thanks before your receive it."

The circle members said aloha to everyone and started packing. Brad and I agreed we'd write each other and share how the class was working in our lives. I laughed and said, "So all those books I read like Norman Vincent Peale on Power of Positive Thinking and Napoleon Hill on Think and Grow Rich really do work. Now all we have to do is decide what it is we want in life. It's like they always say, "be careful what you wish for, you'll probably get it."

11

SPIRITUALITY AROUND THE WORLD

How could anyone be unhappy in Paradise? I was living in one of the most beautiful places in the world. Someone once made the comment that at least one lifetime should be lived on Kauai. Perhaps it was where I was at on my spiritual journey. I was still in the stage of gathering information and attending workshops and conferences. Although I was only a hundred miles from Oahu, the cost to fly there was almost half what it would cost to go to the mainland, making conferences very expensive. But still I went. At work they called me the 'workshop junkie' as I would fly over and have to stay overnight to attend conferences at great expense.

I had already traveled around the world, been on every continent except Antarctica. My travels had taken me from Stonehenge in England, Ayres Rock in Australia, the lost city of

LUTISHA TESAREK

Machu Picchu in Peru, on the Tibetan boarder in Katmandu, the Monastery of 1000 steps at the Golden Triangle Burma Thailand boarder, the 1000 pound golden Buddha in Thailand, the Pyramid and Sphinx in Egypt, Mount Sinai where Moses received the ten commandments, the Rose City of Petra in Jordan, the first Christian Coptic church started by Mark in Egypt, and of course the walled city of Jerusalem.

What was missing was why these places were so special. The usual activities that one does to entertain themselves were meaningless to me. The beach, movies, concerts, parties or socializing had no interest for me anymore. I was really getting worried about myself.

I was finally at that stage, 'Is that all there is?'

I had no real interest in religion, but I wondered constantly about how the universe worked, about why things are the way they are. I got to the point where I couldn't stand small talk, people yammering about everyday problems. It seemed to me, from what I'd been studying, the more you talk about problems, the more you draw them to you.

One day I was in my office and one of the girls came running in saying I had a long distance call from Australia. I picked up the phone and identified myself.

"Natasha, this is Maria from our trip to Alice Springs. Do you remember me?"

"Of course I remember you. How could I forget that memorable bus trip from Darwin to Alice Springs? I though you were headed back for the U.K. after that trip?"

Well I was, but I've stayed with Trevor all this time. Now I'm headed back to the U.K., going to stop in Honolulu and thought I'd stop by and see you."

THE FINAL COMMANDMENTS

I got the time and dates for her visit, and would be glad to talk with someone that had traveled and had some of the same interests I had. I have found that people who have shared interests or travels often become closer to you than someone you've known for years. The more you travel and educate yourself, the harder it is to relate to someone who has stayed in the same situation all their lives.

When I met Maria it was as if none of the years had passed, we just picked up from where she said goodbye to me at the bus station. We reminisced about our time together in Australia.

We arrived at Alice Springs in the early evening. From miles away we could see Ayers Rock. It was majestic, the biggest monolith in the world. Called Ayers Rock by settlers, the ownership of the rock was transferred to the Aborigines of the area and it regained its Aboriginal name of Uluru, which means Great Pebble. Uluru is one of earth's great natural wonders and encountering it for the first time was breathtaking.

Our first excursion the following day was to walk around Ayers Rock. It is a half mile long, one mile wide and rises up to 867 meters above sea level. We learned from our guide that Uluru is a sacred site for the Aboriginal tribes, and has great spiritual meaning. Each feature of the rock has a meaning in 'Tjukurpa' or Dreamtime, the traditional Anangu law that explains how the world was created. The caves in the rock have been decorated with Aboriginal paintings and prehistoric art, some of which indicate such things as the locations of water and other vital information; others were painted for religious purposes and as a means of both storytelling and for a culture with no written language to teach and record its history. Apart from the sheer imposing size of Uluru, what made viewing it so memorable was the fact that as each day passes the rock changes color depending on the light and atmospheric conditions, and never remains the exact same permanent hue. Sunrise and sunset are perhaps the most magical, and it was easy to see why the native inhabitants held this area in such high regard. It is hard to come away from Uluru without feeling enriched by its calm spirituality and sense of permanence.

Later that evening, after an encounter with a man we met named Trevor, we had no trouble getting in to the restaurant we had chosen, or getting the best seat in the Pub. We mentioned how impressed we were with Ayres rock.

Trevor insisted, "Please don't call it that, its proper name is Uluru. It amazes me how someone can say they discovered something that has been there for thousands of years. Sort of like Columbus saying he discovered America. It was named after South Australian premier Sir Henry Ayres, by the white man who discovered it. Until recently large numbers of tourists have visited the rock and climbed it using a rope-and-pole path drilled into the side of the rock. As a result the rock has become eroded. However in 1985 the land on which Ayres rock stands was handed back by the Australian government to the aboriginal inhabitants, the Anangu, descendents of the people who found the rock nearly 10,000 years before the white man. The rock has spiritual significance for the Anangu and they do not climb it. The Anangu now ask tourists to respect the rock by not climbing it, and most tourists comply."

The next day we found out why Trevor was so well respected. He was the number one cowboy of Alice Springs. Although he was half Aborigine, they overlooked that because of his skill in the rodeo. You not only had to compete with horses, but camels

THE FINAL COMMANDMENTS

also. Marie and Trevor hooked up, and she decided to extend her stay.

She told me the incredible story of how she'd spent months in the outback with Trevor with no supplies. He would just know how to get water and food from the barren country. It was truly a spiritual experience. To think you can be in the middle of the desert, with no water or food, and start digging and there's a root for you to eat and water comes out of the barren ground. I shared my experiences in Egypt, and the final commandments of universal laws I was working on. I explained about the three locations for the depositories of the hidden information from Atlantis.

"Natasha, do you think it's a coincidence that I ended up here? It sounds like you and I are on the same path. I actually stopped in Honolulu and did research on Hiram Bingham, who was born in Honolulu. Rumors are he was doing more than looking for the lost city of Machu Picchu in Peru.

"Wasn't he from the missionary family that came to Hawaii?"

"Yes, his grandfather was the first Protestant missionary to come to the Hawaiian Islands. Hiram had a great education, starting with the private schools on Oahu Punahou and Phillips Academy. Then he went to Yale University, University of California, and Harvard University for his postgraduate studies in history and political science his Ph.D. He was a real superman, in every way, even having 11 children. In Connecticut he was Lieutenant governor, Governor, and in the U. S. Senate. He didn't limit himself to the United States either. In WW II he was Vice Counsel in France and helped save 2500 lives by granting Jews visas to escape the country. He served in the

Foreign Service at several Embassies'. Coming home from one
of his posts he visited India and Egypt, and from then on it
seemed like he was searching for something. Someone he was
in contact with in Egypt sent him on a different path of research. Some suggest this is why he became so interested in
South American, and Peru especially. The theory is he wasn't
looking for Machu Picchu when he found it. Perhaps it was
these depositories of information you're talking about. While in
Australia I studied with this group on spirit guides, channeling,
walk-ins, and dreams."

"I've heard of all those things except walk-ins. Is that an
Australian cowboy?" I teased her.

"This is serious business, I guess our world is really in bad
shape. To understand what a walk-in is one first needs to understand that our physical body is not just the body, but also
your soul. In other words we existed as a spirit before the body
we now occupy was born. When our physical body dies we will
continue to exist without it.

The concept of walk-ins seemed to fit in with the cosmic
pattern that when great crises or changes effecting the earth are
coming, illumined entities come from the Once Creative Source
to help mankind. Political, economic, and moral breakdowns
are now occurring. Now is the time for enlightened beings not
to take the regular steps on reincarnation and time-consum-
ing process of birth and childhood. You have a transferal of
egos, allowing a body to be occupied by a superior spiritual
understanding being to serve mankind. When a person feels he
cannot solve his problems on the physical plane, he could allow
a walk-in to occupy his body to accomplish good for humanity.
Since the body is the temple of the soul, it needs to be without

drugs or self-inflicted mortal wounds. Walk-ins want to alert us to potential dangers. Their goals are to forestall World War III, and if enough like-minded people around the world will meditate and work for peace, it will be prevented. All of us have free will, except when it conflicts with universal law. Leaders see advantages to conflicts, such as to divert attention from domestic problems.

There's a famous psychic in Sweden named Bjorn Ortenheim, even your famous Shirley MacLaine has included him in her writings. Bjorn is the walk-in soul of Albert Einstein. He believes the transferal of egos occurred in 1967 during an exceedingly traumatic occurrence in his life.

Look at it this way, each physical body is owned by someone. This person is attached to their body, with a non physical cord, until the body dies. Generally then it is one body one spirit. Multiple people can inhabit the one physical form and this may be termed possession, obsession, multiple personality disorder or whatever. However only one spirit is attached to the body, until physical death of the body.

There is however one exception to this rule. Walk-ins. Walk-ins are people who have spiritual work to do in the material world but for various reasons don't need to spend the time in a physical body growing up. Where a person has finished their life's lessons, and would normally die, in some instances they allow an incoming "walk-in" spirit to be connected to their physical body, that they are leaving behind, instead of them. We still have the case of one physical body, and one spirit attached to it, but in this situation the spirit isn't the one that was with it since birth. Naturally this can then mean that the person may seem to have a major personality change. This is in fact one of the ways one can tell if someone is a walk-in. They will be very much more compassionate, loving, spiritual than before. Walk-ins inherit the memory patters implanted in the physical brain of the body. They claim the spirit of Einstein lives in Bjorn, a Swedish medium, and President Anwar Sadat of Egypt had a walk-in when he was imprisoned. The purpose of this is to help the planet move forward to a higher spiritual perspective. Instant incarnation, as an adult, is a very effective way to get a lot of people into the physical world, helping, in a very short time.

I thought I'd been studying some weird stuff, but this was the weirdest yet!

"I haven't heard of that, but what I'm working on now is channeled books, mainly dealing with scriptures." I continued telling her what I'd learned.

There are several important books that have been channeled. The Moslem's holy book, the Koran, was channeled through Mohammed. He couldn't read or write, yet the holy book was dictated by him. They originally wanted the book to be only in Arabic, so there would be no errors in translation.

Another historical scripture book, The Book of Mormon, is a complex book covering a variety of historical, religious, political, and military events in a variety of ancient communities. The sacred history kept by his descendants covers a span of 600 BC to 400 AD. The Book of Mormon was written by ancient prophets, just as the Bible was written by prophets and apostles of Christ. They claim the writing was done by the spirit of revelation and prophecy. Many authors had contributed directly or were quoted in the final abridgment of ancient records compiled by the prophet, historian, and military leader

Mormon near 400 AD. Joseph Smith, a young farm boy, did the translations.

A book known only to serious researchers is the massive Urantia, which is over 2000 pages. It was first published in Chicago in 1956. The book addresses a broad range of subjects including philosophy, religion, science, sociology, and cosmology. It discusses the origin, history, and destiny of our universe and of humankind; the nature of God; the relationship of God to the world and to the individual; and the life and teachings of Jesus of Nazareth. The Urantia book grew out of trance states of one Wilfred Kellogg, and developed under the direction and editorship of Dr. William Sadler, a psychiatrist who wrote many books himself. In 1911 Sadler found that his brother-in-law, Wilfred Kellogg, went into deep trace states every night. Sadler started questioning Kellogg during these trace states, became intrigued by the claims of the trance personality, and over many years, after countless questioning sessions, and many cycles of revisions, and contributions by a committee of varied size and membership. Sadler printed the immense and bizarre Urantia Book. This book is divided into four parts; The Central and Superuniverses, The Local Universe, The History of our Planet Urantia, and The Life and Teachings of Jesus.

The most interesting in the present day that relates to all religions is A Course of Miracles, which took over 7 years to finish beginning in 1965. Helen Schucman, a Associate Professor at Columbian Presbyterian Medical Center in New York City, states it is the product of 'channeling.' It is supposed to be channeled from Jesus, stating what the real meaning of the Bible is. It is the coming through from a spiritual source which lies beyond the normal world and human consciousness. She grew up in a Jewish-religious environment, but considered herself to be an agnostic in religious matters. Her friend and colleague, Prof. William Thetford, helped with the project by typing out all her notes. The book consists of 365 lessons, 669 pages, and a manual for teachers. The miracle mentioned in the title only happens when we change the way we perceive the world around us, and no longer see ourselves as separate human beings apart from others and God. The premise of the book is that one is either coming from love or fear, and forgiveness is what is needed for love.

Maria commented, "It sounds like some of these manuscripts might have received information from the Akashic Records."

I told her I wasn't sure what that was. She then explained what she had just learned from her studies in Australia.

"The term Akashic comes from a 5000 year old Sanskrit language which means "hidden library." This secret hall of records, known as the Akashic Records, can be revealed by diving into the subconscious mind in a deep state of meditation. The Akashic may be better understood in our technologically advanced world as a type of internal Universal Wide Web, where anyone can access the information freely about anybody.'

The information you'll find in an Akashic Reading is much more than a psychic reading, it is a glimpse into your Soul's path and destiny. We each have access to this information because we are each intimately connected to the Universe, yet sometimes the mind becomes very busy and blocks the connection to this infinite internal database. The Akashic is real. It is a subatomic energy field of quantum particles and waves of information, which are found within everything and everyone in this Universe. It is the informational highway that connects

THE FINAL COMMANDMENTS

all people and things. The Akashic Field of energy is found within each situation you are in. We are all tightly woven into the Universal web of consciousness, this is the doorway into the Akashic. When we tap into and open this subconscious connection, we can pull up specific information about any soul journey, in any place or time in history.

It's stored through your full birth name and birth date. Your information comes through a certain special frequency of energy that is completely different and unique in vibration from anyone or anything in the Universe. It acts like a fingerprint, which is embedded and encoded into the Akashic, thus showing up as your personal Akashic Record. This is your soul's "book of knowledge" or database of information containing the most important and vital information about your soul's mission, purpose and journey in this lifetime. The future is not set in stone, and the more we can realize who we once were, the easier we can re-create who we are today and will be tomorrow.

I see this Universe as a huge beautiful playground which has no boundaries on time or space. By accessing this Akashic Record information we can learn how to help others, and ourselves. The secret to tapping into the ancient Akashic Records is found by entering into an extremely deep and meditative mindset. The Akashic exists at the subconscious level, the state of awareness just before you wake up in the morning or right as you're falling asleep. Only through a deep state of meditation can one bridge the gap and read what's in this massive informational databank without losing consciousness and falling asleep. When we step beyond our normal chattering ego-based mindset and into the silence, we can hear, see and feel this information as if God himself were whispering it to us.

LUTISHA TESAREK

Finding your personal Akashic Record is similar to tuning your car stereo to a particular channel or radio frequency. Your soul sends out a specific "signature" frequency that you can feel, and then the data starts being transmitted from your Akashic Record. Perhaps this "book" is written in energy, or "etched in the ethers." In reality the Akashic Record is storage in consciousness that is everywhere present, just as with the DNA genetic code being present everywhere in your physical body. I believe that exceptional men like Leonardo da Vinci, Galileo Galilei, and Isaac Newton had tapped into the Akashic Records and this is why their knowledge was so far ahead of their time.

Channeling is different from the accessing Akashic Records as another person intercedes for you. According to a recent Gallup poll, 9% of Americans believe in channeling. Channeling is a process whereby an individual, the "channeler", claims to have been invaded by a spirit entity which speaks through the channeler. Actress Shirley MacLaine and the ABC television network gave this modern version of ghosts speaking through a medium a modicum of credibility. In 1987, ABC showed a mini-series based on MacLaine's book 'Out on a Limb', which depicts MacLaine conversing with spirits through channeler Kevin Ryerson.

Channeling means thoughts conveyed have passed through someone's own brain. This process could have modified them, which could occur in channeled books. It may be noteworthy that in French, the word for conscience, our guardian against sin, and consciousness are one and the same.

The channeler, who is a medium, first brings himself or herself in to a totally relaxed meditative state, what we may know as a trance. They then allow themselves to become neutral to

THE FINAL COMMANDMENTS

allow another being or entity to take control over their personality. Essentially you, your own personality, are out to lunch and another spirit takes over your mind and body.

We stayed up all night exchanging ideas and information from workshops and conferences we had been a part of. I knew I would truly miss Maria when she left. After she left there was an emptiness I couldn't explain. My thirst for knowledge and being around kindred spirits on the same path left a hole in my heart.

I started flying to the Kansas City area for classes from Unity School of Christianity. They seem to be the closest to my belief system. The one thing I had always done was listen to that inner voice. It had told me this was not the place for me, I must advance at a faster pace. No one could believe I would leave paradise, with just five years till retirement, and go on some spiritual journey. It didn't make sense economically or professionally either; it only made sense in my heart.

The next few years were spent living at a Yoga and Health Center, and finishing my studies to become a teacher and counselor. I hadn't been back to Kansas except for visits since I left decades ago. My brother and sister lived on a lake only 100 miles from Unity. When I went to visit and was walking around the lake, I saw a For Sale sign on one of the cottages. It had been empty for four years due to a death, and three of the rooms weren't really usable. I was tired of dragging boxes around, and the price was right. The little voice inside just spoke to me, telling me this is the place. I didn't understand this. Why would isolation from everything I cared about be where I was supposed to be?

LUTISHA TESAREK

A few months after I settled, a letter arrived from Monk Arsenios. It had two forwarding addresses on it. Every time I had moved, I had left forwarding addresses, and apparently someone had held on to an old address and forwarded it. Talk about the Universe working in mysterious ways. Otherwise, it would have been in the dead letter file.

When I opened it, I read those few words that would take me on my final journey; "It is time......."

12

—

THE FINAL COMMANDMENT

I had fallen asleep while go-
ing through my life story looking for the connection with the
Universal Laws and Final Commandments. We had a stop over
in London for two hours. I was looking through a magazine
and I heard a familiar voice behind me say, "You must had
drank from the Nile, you seem to always be returning." I turned
around and there was Vern! I couldn't believe after all these
years I would run into him again. Then of course I realized
there are no coincidences, and this was no accident. I started to
ask him about himself and he pulled me away from the crowd
and started walking me down the corridor. He hadn't changed
any, and from is actions, apparently he was in the same field.
He quickly started his anxious message. "Don't look at me, look
straight ahead as if we're just walking side by side. I just had to

let you know the reason you had to leave Egypt didn't have to do with the embassy. It had to do with research you were doing on the original Alexandria Library, the Nag Hammadi Library, and St Catherine Monastery. I can't figure out what that was about, unless it was some stolen or hidden antiquities. Anyway, you haven't been on a list since you left Egypt. Apparently you don't seem to be a threat to anyone now. Whatever you were researching someone didn't want the information to be shared. I still wouldn't stay in Egypt too long this time, just in case." I kept waiting for some personal note, and when he didn't speak for sometime, I glanced over and he was gone! No wonder they call them spooks.

I thought back about my research and what could have been a threat. I tried to think of something so important that someone would want me dead rather than let my research be published. At the time I was researching the material at the original Alexander Library I couldn't understand any real importance that Jesus had left a sample of his DNA. The bible has been edited, but still many believe all statements in the Bible are literally true. If you had actual proof that parts of the Bible are not true, it could change the mindset of the world. It wasn't until a few years ago that The Da Vinci Code was written and upset the Vatican. It made drastic suggestions that Jesus married and had a child, which would leave a bloodline to follow. Part of this research was from the Nag Hamadi Library, which suggest also that woman had a larger roll in the church than acknowledged. It started the ordinary hypnotized population to think on their own. Da Vinci lived in the era where if you dared think other than the church you were condemned and burned at the stake. Because of this

THE FINAL COMMANDMENTS

he devised a code system in his writings and paintings to pass on the information. Perhaps the organization knew of the hidden Commandments that would give people back their power and not be controlled by religion and governments. Hopefully this meeting will answer many of these questions.

When I returned to the plane I started reviewing my past. Actually at each change in my life I could see where the use of the laws were applied. I came out of my few hours of rest because of the announcement the Pyramids could be seen on the left side of the plane. How many times had I looked out at wonder of this sight? Now it meant so much more since I'd studied the true meaning of the Pyramids.

I had barely stepped through the glass door at Customs when someone called my name. It was a diplomat from the Swedish Embassy.

"Madam Natasha, so good to see you again. I met you at St. Catherine's Monastery when our Ambassador's wife was visiting." I looked at him again. I remembered him.

"Madam, I know you have a very important meeting, and since some of our diplomats are attending, we arranged your transportation" he answered very diplomatically.

I thought, "You're back in Egypt, everybody knows your business before you do."

He took my passport and went into a VIP office and was out in five minutes. I've never seen anything done that fast in Egypt.

We went right out the door to a Mercedes with the Swedish diplomat flag on it. We only went about two miles and pulled over to where some smaller planes were waiting.

"We'll fly to the desert on a smaller plane. I'm sure you'll agree this will be easier than an eight hour bus trip." I shook my head yes. Maybe I could sleep while I'm on the plane.

When we went up the ramp I noticed the plane had the Saudi flag on the side. We must be traveling in high circles! The plane was divided with curtains so you couldn't see the other passengers. A hostess came right away with a menu. It was five star all the way. After the meal I was offered a tea that would help me relax and rest during the trip. I probably didn't need it, but I didn't want to offend my host. The tea was very sweet and tasted wonderful. The last thing I remember was the humming of the engines and the hostess putting a blanket over me. I could smell jasmine, it smelled so good. It was hard to force my eyes open. The first thing I saw was stripped walls, with a pole in the center of the room going to the top, like a circus tent. Yes, that's it, a tent. I was still dreaming. I laid there waiting to wake up, but nothing happened. I just kept observing everything around me. We have a group that meets once a week on analyzing your dreams and I was trying to remember everything I'm supposed to recall.

Suddenly someone was in the dream with me. The flap opened and the lovely hostess was bringing me fruit and tea.

I smiled at her and said "This dream has gone on along time, I'm trying to analyze the meaning."

She replied very sweetly, with a very British accent, "Actually it's not a dream. You were so tired we just let you sleep and put you to bed in here." I looked around again, I was definitely in the desert somewhere. I asked to see Suliman or Monk Arsenios. She said the meeting was just getting ready to start and it would have to wait until after that. She'd be back in fifteen minutes to get me. Then she left.

What a weird dream. I pinched myself, ate the fruit, and got up and walked around. I seemed to have control of my movements. I pulled back the corner of the tent and saw a beautiful oasis with a compound of many tent structures. The hostess was right beside me.

"Are you ready to go?"

I pinched myself again. I was trying to think of other things I did to wake up from a dream.

We were all sitting around on the ground Bedouin style. Each of us had on the same garments, long, white galabeyya's. I was pinching myself to see if I was still dreaming. Now I know how Shirley MacLaine felt in her movie "Out on a Limb" when her spiritual partner started talking about flying saucers. She didn't want to get mixed up in anything that far out either. We both have the same birthday, so maybe we're both suppose to be out on that limb.

I looked around at the other participants. I was glancing at their faces to see if I recognized anyone. The first lady I glanced at looked familiar, but I didn't really recognize her. I went to the next face, and was going to go to the next and had to stop. It was the lady that took me to the Pension my first trip to Egypt! What a coincidence.

Then I looked back at the first lady. My heart stopped! She was the lady I met at St. Catherine's Monastery, one of the judges for the Nobel Peace Prize. I shut my eyes. I wanted this to be over. I pinched myself again. I'd heard of hallucinations, and was trying to remember if I'd eaten anything unusual, something with a mushroom in it.

I looked around at the other participants again. As I studied each person, I realized there was some connection through research! I recognized the Professor from the Nag Hamadi Library that I did my research with on my second trip to Egypt. Next to him was the previous Minister of Saudi Arabia. I used to watch him on Face The Nation all the time, sitting there calmly moving his prayer beads smiling while they accused him for the oil prices being so high. I had done a research project on him in business school. I told Katie my daughter I thought he was handsome and jokingly said I was going to the Middle East and work after I graduated. She used to call me long distance and say, "Hey Mom, your boyfriend the Sheik is on 60 Minutes, better turn your TV on."

I had to shut my eyes again, I was connecting to everybody. This was way past coincidence. I realized now there had been some mistake. I had nothing to contribute to these world leaders. There was absolutely nothing special about me.

An elderly gentleman about seventy years old introduced himself as Professor Mark Stevens and started to speak.

"I'm sorry to call you here on such short notice. But it has come to our attention that the energy mass is so out of balance, if nothing is done, the governments will have this world as we know it destroyed. No longer can you drop a bomb in one location and not affect the whole structure of the world. The governments have the people in so much fear they just believe whatever they do is correct. We must make the average person aware that they can have a say in the way their world is run.

"I am going to ask you five questions that I want you to be thinking about throughout the conference. 'What if everyone could read each other's thoughts? What if there was a depository of all the information in the universe that we could tap into anytime we wished? What if the information we have based all our decisions on was incorrect? What if we could have world peace just by thinking it? What if all of you are connected in other ways than research, like an ancient bloodline? I believe your answers to these questions will be different by the end of the conference than they are at this moment."

"You are here, at St. Catherine's Monastery, the place where Moses received the Ten Commandments. Perhaps as you ponder the questions and the reasons you were chosen to be here, you will receive the Final Commandment."

He continued with the rules for this conference. "You were each chosen for the special information you can contribute to this conference, or a special talent. All of you are interconnected in someway. Some of you have even met, or been connected through research. Many were considered, but you are the chosen. There were four criteria for you to be chosen.

"First and foremost, you all realize the danger our world is in because of the neglect of our governments, misinformation being spread, and the abuse of religions. Each of you has stated you want to contribute to bringing our world back in balance.

"Second, you have all studied the same research and understand the problems, so we won't have to spend precious time educating you. We have given some of you many years to understand and accept these concepts that we must convey to the masses.

"Third, you each have special knowledge or talents that are needed for us to complete the project. You have each chosen this in your soul evolution. Each of you has agreed in a previous life that you would work together for the betterment of the world in this lifetime.

"The fourth criteria you will discover at this conference."

I heard the leader's voice again. Even though I'd shut my eyes, I couldn't shut out his voice.

"Some of you are still unsure of the information you have studied, and have not experienced certain things. I assure you, by the time you finish the conference, everything you've read will be understood."

He went on with more rules. My mind drifted to how it wasn't possible I was really here. There was no way I could be the correct person for this task, for this workshop. I was going to sneak out. I would explain that they had chosen the wrong person. I was sure when I spoke with the leader after this meeting this could be straightened out. I was feeling better about the situation, it was a mistake.

As we all separated I wanted to catch up our leader, and explain there was a mistake here. I rushed after him and kept saying, "Professor, Professor." I knew he could hear me.

He stopped in his tacks. "I'm sorry my instructions were not clear, the rest of the evening is for study." He turned again to walk away.

"But I have a right to know," I said. He turned, no emotion in his face, "Know what?" I couldn't ask him all the questions I wanted to, I felt so foolish. I was the only one not obeying instructions.

"Where's Monk Arsenios? That's why I'm here."

He actually smiled, his look now was of a kind, gentle man. "No, Natasha, you're NOT here to see Monk Arsenios. You're here to complete your spiritual journey, your contract for this life. There is no mistake, there is no coincidence, and you are here for a reason. In regards to you not being special, just because the others are famous and have published important papers, does not make your talents less important. You will understand later why you were selected. I was the one who cast the vote to choose you."

He laughed. He turned and said as he walked away. "You can stop pinching yourself; you're here to stay. However, since you insist, I'll give you your challenge early. If you recall, I said you are here to complete your spiritual journey by helping to heal the world. Healing the world begins with The Final Commandment. Each of you has the same assignment. The question is, and your challenge is, 'How will you do that?"

The Professor was correct. After the conference it all did fit together, and time was of essence.

I discovered that the final criteria for our being chosen was DNA. Through all our reincarnations, this group of people survived together as a group. Although Jesus was part of the DNA line, the group actually started with Atlantis, thousands of years before.

When I returned to my tent there was a letter on my bed. I knew it had to be about Monk Arsenios. I didn't know what to expect when I opened it. "Dear Natasha, I am very proud of your soul evolution. You know I would be there if I could. I'm working with a group and our energy level is so high, that if even one of us leaves it would through us off balance. You will probably be forming your own group soon. For myself, I don't care. My soul is ready to leave. But I know you have grandchildren and want to save this planet. Just so you know there was no mistake with you being chosen, you had a great-great aunt that went to Paris to study art. She fell in love with a Count and they had a child. None of your family knew about it. A few years later she adopted the child through the church. So, you really are a chosen one. My thoughts will always be with you." I know he was telling me he wouldn't see me again on earth. I didn't want to let him go.

I kept remembering the Professor's last words to me. "If you recall, I said you are here to complete your spiritual journey by helping to heal the world. Each of you has the same assignment. The question is, and your challenge is, how will you do that?"

Mine is by sharing my experiences and research through a book. This book. As a librarian, what else could I do?

Now I understand why my cottage on the lake turned up when it did. I've been researching and trying to write for several years. I realized I needed all distractions taken away. I've unplugged the TV and only leave my place once a week to shop.

I want people to realize they can make a difference. Using thoughts and meditation, one person can change the world. Many people thinking the same thoughts and meditating or praying about the same issue can change the Universe!

We have only a small window of opportunity to stop this spiral of violence which governments are causing. The ordinary person has just given up, thinking the most they can do is vote. We have to challenge not only that kind of thinking, but also we have to challenge our government and those who represent us.

Several countries are challenging their governments when they know there is wrongdoing. Since the United States is the most dangerous country now, with its war stockpile and warlike ways, it needs to be challenged also. The Universal Law of

THE FINAL COMMANDMENTS

Self-Destruction: total success tends to destroy itself has been proven over and over in the capitol.

I challenge first the politicians. You know there's something very wrong with our system. Each time you are elected, you have to pay out millions of dollars and then you're under control of the contributors. Take back your control, and your conscience. You each have the power to change the dynamics of our system. It will take courage, but you will be the true patriot and hero. Declare yourself an Independent. Take the power away from the Republican and Democrat's, and give it back to the people. Remember in 2000 when just one man had the courage to switch and the power structure changed? Give the power back to the people where it belongs, not the parties. Stop voting to waste our resources on useless military projects. Find ways to solve differences with other countries through negotiations.

My next challenge is to each and every human being. Stop living in fear, and switch to love. Your thoughts create tomorrow, so you must project and manifest what you want, not what you do not want. We can no longer trust or rely on our government to make decisions for us. We must take the time to challenge everything they say, every vote they make. Use your vote to really count. If you don't like what they're doing, vote them out. Start early to make sure your vote counts. Demand a paper for each vote, and help do away with the Electoral College.

The key to peace creation is the experience of Transcendental Consciousness, the direct experience of the unified field of natural law, a state of inner peace. Join a group to make your ideas more powerful. The power of peace-creating groups to decrease warfare and terrorism has been tested repeatedly. The results produced by temporary peace-creating groups have been consistently positive. With just 1% of the population correctly meditating, we can bring down the conflicts in the world.

I believe the most important thing a person can do is listen to their inner voice, and strengthen it through meditation. Praying is talking to God, meditating is listening.

The Final Commandment is LOVE. Think peace and love! Think, pray, and meditate peace and love, and together we will heal our world!

ISBN 141206736-7